AFTERWORDS

Also by W. D. Jackson

Then and Now:

Then and Now – Words in the Dark (Menard Press, 2002)
From Now to Then (Menard Press, 2005)

Selections from *Opus 3*:

Boccaccio in Florence and Other Poems (Shearsman Books, 2009)
A Giotto Triptych (Shoestring Press, 2014)

AFTERWORDS
Or: Occupying No-Man's-Land

(from *Then and Now – Opus 3*)

W. D. JACKSON

Shoestring Press

All rights reserved. No part of this work covered by the copyright herein may be reproduced or used in any means – graphic, electronic, or mechanical, including copying, recording, taping, or information storage and retrieval systems – without written permission of the publisher.

Printed by imprintdigital
Upton Pyne, Exeter
www.imprintdigital.net

Typeset by types of light
typesoflight@gmail.com

Published by Shoestring Press
19 Devonshire Avenue, Beeston, Nottingham, NG9 1BS
(0115) 925 1827
www.shoestringpress.co.uk

First published 2014
Copyright © W.D. Jackson 2014

Cover illustration: Francesco de Goya, 'Ravages of War', from *The Disasters of War* (1863)

ISBN 978-1-910323-11-3

CONTENTS

Prologue: The Curse   3

1 The Carpenter's *Cook's Tale. Or:* Blindman's Buff   5

2 François Villon: Two Extracts from *The Testament*
    i   *Ballade ("Dictes moy ou, n'en quell pays")*   27
    ii   *"Puis de papes, roys, filz de roys"*   28

3 Jove's New World – A Post-Renaissance Picture Gallery   33

4 Heinrich Heine: Two Poems on the History of Religion
    i   Almansor   37
    ii   Princess Sabbath   41

5 Self-Portrait as a White-Collar Worker (4) – Afterwords
    i   Working for the Enemy   49
    ii   Stephanskirchen (1)   50
    iii   after jandl   61
    iv   Death and Brandner Caspar   79
    v   Case Studies, 1941-1945   96
    vi   Stephanskirchen (2)   130
    vii   Mary and Martha (Working for Others)   143

Epilogue: Rilke – In the Same River Twice
    i   *Turn*   147
    ii   L'Ange du Méridien   149

Acknowledgements and Notes   151

"After such knowledge, what forgiveness?"

T.S. Eliot

PROLOGUE: THE CURSE

"Enough! or Too much" – *Blake*

*The apple grew like any other fruit
In that ecstatic garden. But they knew –
Or thought they knew – its knowledge was the root
Of greatness. Till in their growing minds it grew
Like nothing else. The snake's experiment
Was programmed to pollute the atmosphere:
The only knowledge gained was fear
Of losing. And in ways they'd never meant
They now seemed bound to suffer. Since their choice
Would only double-bind them if reversed,
They claimed God's blessing – who were clearly cursed –
And soldiered on, attempting to rejoice
In their achievements. And their fate was such
That their first were last and their last were at least
An unsatisfactory, discontented beast
Condemned, by wanting too much, to* want *too much.*

1 THE CARPENTER'S *COOK'S TALE*. *OR*: BLINDMAN'S BUFF

"Ella, rispostogli, il cominciò a guatare…" – **Decameron IX**, v

*"A Cook they hadde with hem for the nones
To boille the chiknes with the marybones…"*
        The Canterbury Tales, General Prologue

A young apprentice once lived in our town,
as clever as a weasel, handsome, brown
as Spanish leather, learning how to be
a painter – signs, mugs, portraits, pots. And he
was quick and wiry, had a shock of curls,
and was so fond of dancing, ale and girls
that he was widely known as *Pete the Reveller* –
as full of lies or tales as any traveller,
as keen on stolen kisses, love and money,
as a bees' hive is sticky-sweet with honey…

Whenever any pageant filled *Eastcheap*,
out of his master's door P.'d look and leap –
and that was that until he'd seen it all,
or sung and had a dance, or kicked a ball,
or found a gang of mates and called them brother,
who found another gang and caused some bother.

When night fell they'd arrange a time to meet
and drink or gamble in some mean back-street,
where there was no mad cap or leather jerkin
who could compete at dice with this young *Perkin* –
who'd ply his merry tool and blow the lot
in 'private' bagnios, if he won or not.

And this was bad for trade.
                      His master started
missing things – tools, wine, takings… Not hard-hearted,
he felt betrayed – then angered. Revel and theft,

it seemed, were front and back, or right and left,
of Peter and, before he'd fully served
his time, he got what he no doubt deserved:
"A rotten apple in a barrel will
rot all the others if left there, until
nothing but worms and grubs remain alive.
I'd say in your case, Peter, at least five
of the seven deadliest worms have long begun
to do their damnedest... And I'm not the one
to pluck them out, although when young I admit
I had some fun myself and went for it
where- and whenever. But you've breached my trust
by stealing from the till. Which means I must
dismiss you, I've no choice. And so – *Get out,
you thieving, greedy, lecherous, lazy lout!* –"

His indignation grew so righteous that
Peter skedaddled like an alley-cat.

But one thief always knows another thief
to help him hoodwink, fleece or bring to grief
the dupes they lend a hand to. Peter sent
one such to fetch his gear, while he himself went
to ground nearby in the small grocer's shop
this friend's wife owned.
                        She had another job
as part-time tart, or closet prostitute.

The shop itself, though, was of good repute,
having become hers when the grocer died...
In fact, her bit of income on the side
was now, since she'd re-married, not much more
than a bad habit: *Laura* was no whore
but, like the Wife of Bath, a provident
house-keeper with a "*likerous instrument*".

Her second husband worked – as part-time pimp
and under-skinker: *Pompey* smarmed, *Why scrimp
and slave*, carissima, *to buy new dresses?*

A cortegiana *in Napoli possesses*
more than great ladies. Usura *on her back –*
she lends one talent but she gets ten back…

Tempted and hooked, the loose and lovely Laura
plied London's oldest trade, and grew no poorer,
keeping her shop as well.
                      The painter's wife
and she had known each other all their lives:
their mothers had been friends. But Laura's father
had died and left them poor. The girls would gather
berries, nuts, flowers to sell from the nearby common.
L.'s mother was a feisty market-woman
and sold herself, shooing them out to play
girls' games – tick, blindman's buff. And to that day
plump *Christiana* bought salt, sugar, flour
from Laura's shop.
                 Her husband, *Christopher*,
knew nothing of their grocer's sideline, which
Christiana tolerated. After such
a very old first husband, who had died
in ecstasies while somewhere up inside
his less than pleasured – widow, who could blame
poor Laura?
           She felt sorry, all the same,
when Pompey beat her: he was slightly mad,
Laura explained, but when not in a bad
temper wept maudlin rivers for the thick
lip or black eye he'd given her, or would lick
and kiss her like a dog… Felt sorry, too,
if some drunk client beat her black and blue –
which Pompey sternly treated as no joke
but, smiler with a knife beneath his cloak
or, more precisely, razor-sharp stiletto
like Sparafucile's, hired by Rigoletto,
bagged the offender and, like Buridan –
first loved, then dumped, in Paris by Queen Jeanne –
floated them down the Mincio, Thames or Seine
to ensure they'd never get a girl again.

Two things made Laura's husband feel *cornuto* –
a violent client or a love-lorn suitor…

"*Coraggio, cara!*" he then softly said,
and slid off back to work at the Boar's Head,
whose host, Ned Quickly, for a small inducement,
helped gull another Dick for L.'s seducement.

Not that she told her neighbours much of this,
and least of all a housewife like plump Chris,
even when she claimed that Chris made her feel lucky
and loved enough to get a daily fuck – he
wasn't as fit as he'd once been but still
did very nicely thankyou.
                                      Laura would smile
to hear it – but then deftly turn the talk
to safer subjects, such as food or work.

And so it was that Chris heard their false friend
Peter had gone to work in the West End
at a large inn, the Garter, where his uncle
was landlord.
                      Hurrying home, she broke her ankle –
a complicated fracture, which made life
painful for months. Although Chris loved his wife,
this twist of fortune got on both their nerves.
Even *if* she'd somehow got what she deserved,
Peter was gone and *Jill*, their hapless maid,
was pregnant. Chris, who for long weeks was laid
in splints across the bed, would pester Chris
to fetch and carry, fix that or buy this…

So that, one afternoon, the painter stood,
in an impatient, irritable mood,
at Laura's, clutching a long list of shopping
his wife had ordered.
                          Laura had just been swapping
tit for tat with a client.
                      Her eyes shone

as, without thinking, she now turned them on
this man with paint and egg-white on his shirt.

Before he knew it, Chris began to flirt
and, though for twenty years he had had eyes –
well, almost – for Chris alone, stared in surprise
as a sunbeam lit up Laura's auburn hair
and long bare milk-white neck. Gasping for air,
he felt her brush against him with her breasts.

She soon forgot him. He could hardly rest
until he'd found a reason to come back.
He bought a bag of nuts. "Mind you don't crack
your eyeballs," Laura laughed, who'd heard meanwhile
of Christiana's fall.   Her loose-lipped smile,
which looked (she couldn't help it) more than naughty,
now made the painter feel, though long turned forty,
like a young tyro with a loaded brush,
unsure if he should jab, dab, pull or push –
which made him (nor could he) look such a fool
that Laura very softly flicked his tool,
explaining hers was not a knocking shop,
and if he thought it was, he'd better stop
before she flicked him harder.   The next time
that Chris went shopping, the whole pantomime
was viewed by Peter through the window – who
had got his eye on loose-lipped Laura, too,
but was afraid of Pompey, who distinguished
clients from lovers/rivals, and extinguished
the flames of love (P. knew), if they appeared,
with mezzogiorno ruthlessness.   He leered,
You fancy her as well, old man, I see,
but frowned and bit his thumb-nail enviously
as Laura, making bedroom-eyes, now led
Chris down into her cellar, where a bed
lurked in a curtained niche (P. also knew) –

scented by apples – spices – *Oh no you
don't, you old lecher! Or not yet*, he thought,
and clattered in – just as his master brought
a solid sack of walnuts up the ladder.

Pete smirked to see Chris look, abruptly, sadder –
but passed the matter off with "Where's Pompey?
– I was supposed to meet him here today…
And no hard feelings, *maestro*. Why not let
bygones be bygones?" And so on.
                                   To cut
etc., P. contrived a clever plan
to get his master kicked out too (*Like man,
like master*) – first of all, ingratiating
himself with Chris, and then negotiating
a deal for him to paint and re-design
his prosperous uncle's crudely daubed inn-sign,
as well as to replace in sets of ten
his mugs, bowls, plates, which P. collected when
each batch was ready.
                         All of which dispelled
their troubled past.
                         Even Chris (still laid up) quelled
the qualms of vague mistrust she'd always had
regarding Peter, who had something bad
(she feared) about him – not that she could prove
anything now – whereas Chris, being in love,
trusted him more, and life in general, too,
gaily re-painting London town sky-blue
with rose-pink borders and a golden frame.

Middle-aged men, L. mused, are all the same,
including artists, who are even blinder
than most – until some hard-and-fast reminder
of who's who, what's what, rips the blindfold off.
And then they realize *Enough's enough…*
This artist, though – she guessed – was narcissistic
and easily flattered (Laura was realistic
about her friends): a well-heeled master, too –

wealthier than most with whom she had to do,
and more polite… And yet she didn't want
too much attention to her famous *queynte* –
which, like the Wife of Bath's, was highly praised
by all and sundry – such that she'd lose face,
or start perhaps (a chastening thought) to seem
a *Mistress Overdone*. She'd always creamed
the biggest spenders off, while too much screwing
was also dicy if it stopped her doing
her duty to her husband's satisfaction –
which easily caused a 'slightly mad' reaction –
and could, as she well knew, be just as dull
as not enough, like feeling over-full
of fish on Friday…
                    What with thoughts like these,
all L. did next was flirt a bit and tease
her new admirers, master more than man –
whose 'love', though, far from hampering his smart plan,
propelled it forward with the acrid power
of jealousy, whereas Chris felt by now
confused and slightly vexed by L.'s reaction
on top of Chris's agonized inaction.

At Peter's reckless age, he'd run as wild
a riot, or wilder. As an only child,
he'd blown his father's money even faster
than Peter had blown his, and riled his master
with similar "*litel japes*"… In fact, they soon
found things to laugh about.
                              One afternoon,
when Peter came to fetch a batch of plates
which hadn't yet been fired, and had to wait,
the painter (who had no idea at all
that he was fooling with a jealous rival
for Laura's favours) started cracking jokes
about the sort of Judy bloke-ish blokes
crack jokes about, and passed a rude remark
about their friend – one bird who, for a lark,
he'd love to get his hands on…

                          Now P. had
a clear enough idea how sad or mad
Laura might make a man and, seizing this chance
to call the tune and lead old Chris a dance,
confided how he'd known her for some time –
a merry widow, and still in her prime,
though Pompey's foreign or half-mad distinctions
had led (he'd heard) to more than one extinction
not just of hope but of the very hoper.
They should have been content to pay and grope her!
But why not try a gift? As long as he
was – or, at any rate, appeared to be –
only a punter (wasn't that the word?),
Pompey would turn a half-blind eye. Absurd,
but there it was.
                    Chris stared. Nonplussed at first
by this unwelcome news, he inwardly cursed
Italian migrants and, above all, Pompey
for wiving, thriving, getting in the way,
corrupting English girls, above all Laura,
who had no need, with so much going for her,
to play that sort of game. And surely wouldn't,
unless she had to. Pompey probably couldn't
earn anything like enough to make ends meet:
a *little* gift, perhaps – sweets to the sweet –
offered discreetly, then, could not do much
real harm – and might well help…
                                       Amazed that such
a lovely woman should have stooped so low
and married a mere tapster/gigolo,
he even quizzed his wife (who'd know) on how
she'd lost her standing.
                            "Well, since when have you
troubled your head, my dear, with Eastcheap's wives?"
she smiled – but winced with pain: "We get the lives
we earn. And even the luck. Anyway, Laura
and her old mother kept on getting poorer –
until she married, well, an older man…
After her mother died, she carried on

with other men behind his creaking back.
One night it creaked so much she heard it crack,
and that was that. She inherited the shop
and all that he possessed. But why, then, stop
playing the games she'd started? Times were hard…
Pompey, as tapster and as part-time bawd,
was not, you see, so very far below her…"

But Chris saw Laura as the topmost *flower*
of female beauty. As his wife suspected.
– Trouble, in fact, was almost to be expected
under the circumstances. Still in pain,
she tried to move her legs – but failed again
to part them without wincing.
                              And quite soon
her husband swinked elsewhere all afternoon.

Now L. had always thought the mouse which had
only one hole was soft or thick in the head –
You're cat-food once the cat discovers it! –
and made full use of every hole or slit.
– The little gifts Chris brought, like magic charms,
were all it took to have her in his arms.

To inflate his self-respect, she then requested
some work of Chris's own – a tried and tested
method with even the average artisan,
and Chris was an artistic, cocksure man –
to go with his more mundane contributions,
which helped her pay their bills.
                                  Two loud intrusions
by neighbours shouting *Shop!* and the constant threat
of Pompey blundering in on them, soon led
to Peter's slyly offering to keep nix,
while Laura taught her ageing dog new tricks.
But, standing like a lemon in the shop,
P. fancied he could hear them on the job;
and, once, when Pompey banged in with a fellow-
Italian for some *vino* from their cellar,

felt sourly tempted to tear down the sign
which told him Laura had a paying client.
Pompey was an Italian, after all –
and, surely, this might serve as Chris's fall?
But, gambling on an even worse disgrace,
he cut off his nose again to spite his face,
and Pompey stamped off with an angry frown…

When Laura smirked, "Don't let it get you down,"
P. threw her such a furious glance that she
suddenly felt afraid.
                         Before long he
was also allowed to leave her little *donnés*,
consisting largely of ill-gotten moneys.
And Laura assured him, as he grasped her hips
and kissed her hot and slightly puffy lips,
that he was so much stiffer than his master –
who once or twice had had a slight disaster
and was much less attractive than he dreamed.

Peter mistrusted Laura, but she seemed
in fact to find him sexier than old Chris,
whom once she stood up in his favour.
                                       This
pleased and excited Peter rather more
than he admitted – L. was only a whore,
when all was said and done – and drove him on
to visualize the details of his plan,
which might, he now perceived, also deter
Laura from screwing Chris – or him from her –
depending on which ways their bit of fun
turned nasty.
                   Very soon the deed was done.
When Chris's leg was healed enough for her
to hobble round on, Peter showed her where
a basement window in the grocer's yard
revealed her husband and the grocer, hard
at work on a large bed in a dark corner.

Pete whispered that he'd felt he had to warn her –
although he'd hesitated, as their friend –
and yet it would have come out in the end,
as these things do…
                        Now Chris was badly shocked
to see her husband's straining body locked
below her in a passionate embrace
with someone else's. Hiding her white face,
she stared between cramped fingers – till a cry
of angry pain caused cock and hen to fly
apart as quickly as if the bed had burst.

They glimpsed poor Chris and – cowering as if cursed –
shielding their nakedness, like Adam and Eve
shut out of Eden – saw her quickly leave
the little window vacant, like the eye
of heaven.
            Then silence.
                            A whole week went by
while Peter waited for a bigger bang –
and then two weeks…
                        But they could all go hang,
for all he cared.
                    L. said there'd been a fuss,
which ought to leave "more time", she smiled, "for us" –
but had less time than ever.
                                Then, one day,
when L. had let him have – for once – his way,
fearing his temper and the angry glow
which filled his face whenever she said no,
he bounced off Chris while sidling idly out.

The look she shot him left him in no doubt –
("*My sone, keep wel thy tonge, and keep thy freend:
a wikked tonge is worse than a feend*") –
of where he stood.
                    He eavesdropped at the door –
could hear excited voices, not much more,
until the cellar trap-door banged. Was this

some sort of scrap at last?
                              So as not to miss
the teeth and claws, he scuttled round to the yard
and squatted by the window, breathing hard,
craning his neck to sneak a better look,
and saw them – *laughing*.
                              Then Laura, smiling, took
a black silk blindfold from her box of tricks –
which Chris admired – plus several hand-carved pricks,
seeming to offer them. But Chris declined
shyly. She was about to change her mind
when Laura spotted Peter.
                              Off he scurried,
though not before Chris too had glimpsed his worried
and puzzled face.
                              Laura so far had not
tumbled to Peter's sly Boccaccian plot,
but Chris, in tears, now told her how she'd come
to get a bird's-eye-view of Chris's bum
between her parted knees. And straight away
Laura decided that the only way
to rid themselves of Peter was to lie
to Pompey – how he'd sworn to God he'd die
if Laura didn't give him love, refusing
to accept the simple deal (beyond her choosing)
whereby the only 'love' she had for him
was if he coughed up coins to grease her quim…

She knew exactly what to do and say
to egg her husband on. The following day
was his young rival's last. So much for Peter.

As for nice Chris, whose husband never beat her,
who craved no other, nor a better man
(even if he'd fallen for Pompey's courtesan) –
or so she claimed – who was an honest woman,
L. had been moved not only by their common
memories, however much they'd grown apart
in matters of the body and the heart,

but how she'd come to ask her if she'd *help*
and not to tear the hair from off her scalp,
or scratch her cheeks, or slit her pretty nose,
screaming it from the roof-tops to expose
her guilt – as peeping Peter still expected
while crouching at the key-hole undetected…

All Chris had said was Chris had sworn / would swear
not to return to Laura's. But hot air,
she sighed, cost nothing, and she was afraid
of what L. knew, that most men's fifth decade
made them less faithful, not to say more foolish,
while mid-life hard-ons can be downright mulish.
And so, though pained, she'd swallowed her hurt pride,
begging her childhood friend to take her side
if and when Chris went back and broke his word:
she loved him, which was utterly absurd,
perhaps – but there it was. L. didn't need
the money, surely? Or would soon succeed
in finding someone more to her real taste –

At this point Laura, clasping her plump waist,
had kissed her mouth to close it: "To my mind,
it's lust," she blinked, "not love at all that's blind" –
and placed a sticky piece of candied ginger
between her friend's hot lips, and licked her finger…
"Like lots of men, he's half-blind anyway. –
Do you remember how we used to play,
as adolescent girls, at blindman's buff
with some dumb boy-o, who'd get biffs enough
before he snatched a blouse or groped a skirt?
Sometimes we'd kick him where it really hurt,
or spin him round so quick it made him dizzy,
or strap one boot to a chair to keep him busy.
And what was his reward for all of this?
To give the girl he caught a blindman's kiss.
We were too shy to let him see whose mouth
he had his tongue in. Well, goodbye to youth,
but let me show you something – "

                        And they went,
banging the trap-door, down into the scent
of Laura's spicy cellar.
                    Laura knew
that men like Chris imagine if they screw
another woman in another bed
the wife they have at home must be half-dead.
And nothing either she or Chris could *say*
would make much difference.
                        "But why don't we play
a game of blindman's buff – "
                        She was about
to explain when Peter left them in no doubt
of his ill will by showing his real face
in the same frame he'd used to try and disgrace
his former chief...
                    Well, let him bite his thumb.
Hard-faced, hard-bitten as she had become,
Laura still felt his plan should be frustrated
and Chris returned to Chris – and concentrated
her mind on that...
                    Later, she sent Chris home
with two fine dildos, carved by hand in Rome,
a gift of Pompey's – to be left around
where the old goat her husband would be bound
to spy them.
                    Which he did. One in the hand
of Jill their maid, who didn't understand
the look he gave her, having found it on
their unmade bed.
                    He found the other one
being used by Chris, who felt a pang of shame
but kept her eyes tight shut and sighed and came
as if he wasn't there.
                    She then felt shifty. –
But *how* could he have lived to almost fifty
and not know women get frustrated, too?

Jill railed that you could *talk* till you were blue

between the legs. Look at her new-born child,
whose father hadn't listened to her mild
entreaties to be careful...
                    Jill turned red:
"And then he said he'd fallen in love," she said,
"with someone else."
                    Chris, who'd been fairly sure
P. was the father, wasn't any more –
and felt another pang, but overcame
her stinging tears and, since their little game
of blindman's buff required one other 'girl'
at least for Chris to chase, suggested Jill
might like to play a part in Laura's plan
to help her show her dick-head of a man
how wrong he was.
                    To judge from the fierce light
that flared in Jill's dark eyes, Chris had been right
on several counts – and Jill said, "Count on me!"
nursing her baby, *Jack*, self-righteously...
A fortnight passed.
                    After the interlude
with Laura's dildo, Chris had shown renewed
interest in Chris. But such is the blind power
of what we imagine or expect on our
immediate feelings that, like a cold sword
between them lay the thought that he was bored
compared with when at Laura's.
                    Till at last,
he imagined the main danger was now past –
and, having put L. wise the previous day,
laid the white lies on thick to get away:
Peter had now gone AWOL for some time –
questions were being asked – some feared a crime.
And so, as his ex-master, now his friend,
Chris was invited up to the West End
for jaw-jaw at his well-off uncle's inn,
the Garter, where he'd actually never been –
not even to inspect his own inn-sign
in situ, though he'd heard that it looked fine...

– All this though Chris herself looked fine as ever,
whereas he hummed, "*To one thing constant never*"
as, sure enough, the old temptation grew:
if he could swing it, why not swive with two
lovers, one here, one there? Why should they be
so difficult to cope with separately? –
And various schemes soon filled his swelling head.

Later, when Chris and Laura were both dead,
and Chris and Jill were looking after Jack,
a poet-courtier, dressed in sombre black
and nondescript dark-grey, with goatee beard
and vulnerable eyes, one day appeared
in Eastcheap and commissioned Master Chris
to paint his 'final' portrait.
                                Vis-à-vis
Chaucer – for he it was – who sat so still
that words at once welled up to break or fill
the utter silence, Chris began to tell
his story, starting with that ne'er-do-well
'Peter' *et al* – a cast so nearly the same
as Chaucer's *Cook's Tale* that the one changed name
permitted me to use it as the start,
roughly, of my own story.
                          Easing his heart,
'Chris' (as I've called him) blurted a whole version
of whatever really happened – some distortion
is only human – and, in a single session
less of self-portrait than ersatz Confession,
arrived at Laura's ploy of blindman's buff.

And some of this raw yarn was novel stuff
(an unsubmissive and yet loving wife –
a lily flowering in low London life)
for Chaucer *re* male/female interactions;
but he'd already written his *Retractions*,
preceded by *The Parson's Tale*…
                                He told
most of the story, though, to me – his old

acquaintance – well, I think we can say 'friend',
though he of course was at the upper end
of the overcrowded ladder of the court,
from which he duly toppled, knowing he ought
never to have wasted so much life and time
on the hand- and foot-holds of that slippery climb…

It just so happens he and I would meet
for dinner at the Garter, where young Pete
flourished as ex-apprentice and head-skinker.

Pompey was an occasional fellow-drinker,
a former smuggler and Boar's Head rampallion,
spicing his English with ribald Italian.
After he'd married Laura – "*come Petrarca*" –
his dark, louche face at times looked even darker:
Chaucer would watch ("*he was a good felawe:
ful many a draughte of wyn had he ydrawe
from Bordeux-ward, whil that the chapman sleep.
Of nyce conscience took he no keep.
If that he faught, and hadde the hyer hond,
by water he sente hem hoom to every lond*") –
and sometimes write a few quick phrases, tapping
the ale-house table, sometimes seem to be napping,
but "*Rivo!*" he'd smile – and never miss a thing.

Before his exile, once, our present King
and his tall, skinny ten-year-old son, Hal,
with Sir John Falstaff – now his humorous pal –
rode by as we stepped out.
                        And Bolingbroke
whispered to Falstaff, who flashed back a joke –
at our expence? Well, Chaucer already knew,
or so he claimed, what Henry was up to…

I'd met him on the pilgrimage.
                             For years
I'd worked on Chester quire. Great hopes, great fears…
When Richard came of age, he was promoted

to Clerk of the King's Works. Though he devoted
far too much energy (I thought) to what
others did better, I helped him on a lot
of buildings – some begun by Richard, who
was wasteful, arrogant, but brilliant too,
and open-minded. But at last he fell
a victim to Archbishop Arundel,
a man whom he'd offended many times,
not least by knocking clerics in his rhymes
as scroungers, thieves or wealthy hypocrites,
which got on this rich, worldly cleric's tits.
He had him robbed and badly beaten up –
twice – like a helpless lackey or young cub.
After the *coup*, he was convinced his days
were numbered, though he rented a new place –
I built his library – in the Abbey garden
at Westminster.
                    But nothing now could pardon
his *Tales*, he feared, in the eyes of Arundel.
Still insecure – one month a mere exile,
the next in power – King Bolingbroke and he
demanded hymns of praise, not irony,
or disrespectful fabliaux with fat friars,
summoners, pardoners, monks – all rogues and liars.
The new regime's diktat was *Church and state
dispense the truth*.
                    Laws meant to intimidate
rebellion or revenge were quickly passed.
Free-thinking speech became a thing of the past.
Richard was soon to die, his name disgraced.
Chronicles were censored, manuscripts defaced.

Chaucer, who'd long observed high politics,
remarked, "Next they'll be burning heretics."
Revenge and violence, though, he'd always said,
would heap more dead on those already dead –
and feared the rabid dogs of Civil War
would harry the Dance of Death from shore to shore.

And yet his pale and deeply worried face,
protected briefly from His worrying Grace,
still lit up with delight and, yes, surprise
when telling Chris's story.
                           His tired eyes
closed with exquisite joy – when Chris requested
a further tryst – at what L. had suggested.
She felt so shagged, she coolly shammed, that the best
thing *she* could do was take a well-earned rest.
Pompey suspected everyone. Young Pete,
she'd bet her boobs, had been dispatched to meet
his fellow-revellers in the halls of Hell –

Chris looked her up and down: *What, him as well?*
he didn't say but, slightly less in love,
felt peeved.
              When she suggested blindman's buff
with local wives and 'colleagues', he had mixed
though potent feelings. So a time was fixed
for two days later. Chris could have the one
he caught. Of course, they'd all have nothing on,
including him. The only little rule –
which wouldn't make him feel, she hoped, a fool –
was that he mustn't take his blindfold off,
no matter what, until he'd had enough
of what she guaranteed he'd get more than
could be enjoyed by almost any man,
and left her house. Her friends were part-time, too,
and weren't quite sure yet if he should know who
he'd have his dick in.
                      Laura's way with words
(no metaphoric honey-bees, no birds –
no poetry) had always shocked and charmed him.
Her offer now excited and disarmed him,
reminding him of certain wild week-ends
as a reckless youth – with loose, like-minded friends
at a small private brothel in another
part of the town – arranged by the girls' mother.

– Would L. play too, he'd asked.
　　　　　　　　　　She hadn't planned
to do so, she replied. But, since demand
stimulates growth, "Well, then, if you insist…"
she yielded coyly, though would not have missed
for all the world – nor Jill – the chance to get
her own back for what life and luck had let
men do to them.
　　　　　　　This almost went too far
when Chris got biffed and battered on a par
with his misdeeds, but stopped at last when they
let him catch Chris: "*Ther is namore to seye,
but al that nyght this peyntour wol embrace
his wyf al newe, and kiste hir on hir face,
and up he gooth and maketh it ful tough.
'Namoore,' quod she, 'by God ye have ynough!'
And wantownly agayn with hym she pleyde,
til atte laste thus the peyntour seyde:
'I knowe thy voys!' 'Tehee,' quod she. Anon
she caughte his coillons and they were atoon
agayn. On his owen wyf he leith on soore.
So myrie a fit ne hadde he nat ful yoore;
he priketh hard and depe as he were mad.
This joly lyf han these two loveres lad
til they waxe wery in the dawenynge.*"

They heard the birds outside begin to sing.
The third cock crew.
　　　　　　　　She crooned, "My love, my life,
had you not better go home to your wife?"

Chris laughed out loud: "I *know* your voice! Let's see
your face now," laughing louder still as she
grabbed his soft tool and pulled his blindfold off…

Chaucer concluded with a modest cough,
commenting (when I asked) on how, at last,
making such love can flood and drown the past –
also the future, to which all men come

(but what on earth's the point of looking glum?) –
and is another blindfold, although they,
as lovers, *chose* to wear it from that day,
which made it seem a harmless, happy one…
Death's our last blindfold in that it stays on.
Chris died in childbirth. A late pregnancy
blessed and then blighted unexpectedly
their game of love.
     If turds like Arundel
and Perkin Reveller, who belong in Hell,
stuck up the Devil's arse, don't always get
their sour revenge, the lives and luck we let
accumulate around us still conspire
to show the *more* our hearts and minds desire
the more they suffer. And the more we plan
to win against or screw another man
or men, the more we lose.
       After Chris died,
Laura screwed more and more. She lost her pride,
and then her caution.
       Someone cut her throat.

Pompey was picked up in a rowing boat
beside a tall ship bound for Italy:
"*È morta, è morta!*" he wailed unhappily,
then wept so much he couldn't say a word.

The judge decided he was too absurd
or mad to hang, if guilty, which was not
proved beyond doubt, and gaoled him.
         Pompey's lot
was as odd as Pompey. Chris heard he'd become
a hangman and was known as Pompey Bum…

I went to see Chris later. He remembered
Chaucer's conviction that his days were numbered,
the greyness of his aura, like a veil,
his pleasure, even so, in their 'Cook's Tale'
(which made him think of something in *Boccacce* –

a funny / heartless tale he couldn't place)
and Jill attending to her baby's needs.
He'd sat and smiled – and told his black prayer-beads…
The painter felt oppressed by a sense of sin.
He died soon after and is buried in
St Luke's, of course, the patron saint of all
who leave their mark, like snails, on wood or wall.

2 FRANÇOIS VILLON: TWO EXTRACTS FROM *THE TESTAMENT*

Ballade
("Dictes moy ou, n'en quel pays")

O tell me in which country now
Is Flora, the lovely Roman?
Or Alexander's Thais who
Was Alcibiades' cousin;
Echo who spoke – poor tongue-tied woman –
Where babbling waters pool or flow,
Whose beauty was more than human? –
But where is last year's snow?

Where is the learned Heloise,
For whom they gelded Abelard?
Made him a monk at Saint Denis –
Love pained him long and hard!
And where's the queen who ordered her guard
To tie up Buridan and throw
Him into the Seine like a tub of lard?…
But where is last year's snow?

Queen Blanche who sang – sweet fleur-de-lys –
Like a Siren come again;
Big-footed Bertha, Beatrice, Alice,
And that Amazon who held Maine;
And Jeanne, the good girl of Lorraine
Burnt by the English… Where are they? Oh,
Sweet Virgin Mary, long may you reign:
But where is last year's snow?

If any should ask this week, this year,
Where are they? Where did they all go?
This same refrain is all you'll hear:
Where is last year's snow?

***

("Puis de papes, roys, filz de roys")

The same thing goes for kings and popes,
Their fecund queens, and all their sons –
Buried together with their hopes,
Their power and glory gone.
And won't *I* die, a poor bag-man
From Rennes? Oh, yes. If it please God,
As long as I've had my fun,
I'll rest under any sod.

This world won't last for ever,
Whatever the thieving rich may think –
We're all of us under fate's cleaver,
Any old crock on the brink
Will tell you. Young and in the pink,
He'd josh his wife – his friends – his folks –
But, now, would cause a social stink
If he started cracking jokes.

Obliged to beg or steal or borrow
By heartless Mother Necessity,
He gloomily hopes today that tomorrow
His death will set him free –
And, but for God's commandment, he
(With his back to yet another wall)
Often might have horribly
Put an end to it all!

For if in his youth he made them laugh,
Nothing he says now can or will:
An ancient ape's a horror-and-a-half;
His sour face sucks life's bitter pill.
If he's silent they think he's ill,
Or finally going gaga.
If he speaks he's told to be still:
Who cares for his second-hand saga?

And as for poor decrepit biddies
Without a sou, or fish to fry,
Who see young things with plumped-up diddies
Taking their place on the sly,
They importune God to tell them why
And by what right they were born so *soon!*
But our Lord declines to argufy,
Knowing he'd get the wooden spoon…

I seem to hear the beauty who
Was once an armouress
Wishing their wish which can't come true –
For youth again – like this:
"Ah, why has age crept up, like a fierce
Thief, so soon, to crease my skin?
What stops me now, in my distress,
From doing myself in?

Old age has left me in the lurch
And stripped my beauty of its power
Over merchants, scholars, men of the church:
There wasn't one who wouldn't shower
All that he owned, his widow's dower –
No matter what – on me
For an hour or less than an hour
Of what tramps won't tickle now for free!

I refused it to plenty of men,
Which wasn't especially smart of me,
For the love of a young ex-con
Who never paid my fee.
He fooled me. But – I swear it – he
Was my sweetest taste of honey.
Who cares if he mainly seemed to be
In love with my hard-earned money?

Who cares if he dragged me round the floor
Or kicked me a bit? He couldn't kill
My love. If he'd broken my back or my jaw,

Then asked for a kiss, I'd still
Have given him one with no ill will...
A fat lot *I* got, all the same.
The greedy bully screwed me, until
There's nothing left but the sin and shame.

And he's been dead these thirty years.
But I live on – old, grey and glum.
When I think of the good times – remember, in tears,
What I was and what I've become –
When I look at my naked breasts and bum,
And see my body so very changed,
Poor, dry, meagre, gnarled and numb,
I think I must be completely deranged.

What has become of that lucid brow?
That golden hair, those eyebrows raised
Above my wide-set eyes, aglow
With pretty glances which amazed
The shrewdest; and my straight nose, praised
Together with my shapely ears
And dimpled chin; my face which gazed
With hope into the coming years?

My slender shoulders – oh, and those lips!... –
Long arms, slim fingers, skilled at their trade,
Small boobs, full buttocks, swinging hips –
A fine high arse, as good as made
For the fine art of getting laid;
Those marble loins, that tiny V
Between my powerful thighs, in the shade
Of its own sweet-scented shrubbery?

My forehead's wrinkled, hair's gone grey,
My brows are scurf and my eyes dull
Which flashed hot looks and smiles in their day
At many a lecherous fool;
My nose is hooked like the beak of a gull;
My pendulous ears sprout moss;

My drab skin hardly hides my skull;
My chins are puckered, lips a dead loss.

This is the way our beauty ends:
My arms are short, hands cramped and lean;
My shoulders hunch as my spine bends;
My tits are – pah! – just shrunken skin,
My buttocks as slack, all fallen in.
My cunt? A horror! My thighs? The truth is
Their bones are sticks, not thigh-bones – thin
And blotched with spots, like sausages.

– And that's how we mourn the good old days
Among ourselves, poor senile crones
Who squat on our hams by a small blaze
Of twigs and straw, like bundles of bones
And rags. The fires which light our groans
No sooner flare than they go out…
And we were all so lovely once.
But that's how it is for tart and tout."

3 JOVE'S NEW WORLD – A POST-RENAISSANCE PICTURE GALLERY

"Men say that Giantes went about
  the Realme of Heaven to win,
To place themselves to raigne as Gods
  and lawlesse Lordes therein...
The which as soone as Saturns sonne
  from Heaven aloft did see,
He fetcht a sigh..."
                              Ovid, ***Metamorphoses I***

In most Renaissance paintings of classical subjects – with famous exceptions such as the rape of Chloris in Botticelli's Primavera *or Titian's* The Flaying of Marsyas *– the gods, when they appear, are not only beautiful but seem, in the main, to be benign. And yet in the myths themselves, as recounted in even the better-known ancient literature, Zeus/Jove – or "Saturns sonne" – for example, frequently behaves like a tyrant whose power has gone less to his head than to his organs of reproduction. In fact, reproducing himself in one shape or another seems to have been one of Jove's main ways of passing the time or, in his case, eternity. In the above lines from Arthur Golding's translation of Ovid's* Metamorphoses *(1537), Ovid seems to compress allusions to Saturn and the Titans' attack on their father Uranus, and Jove's attack on Saturn, into an (unsuccessful) attack on Jove himself. Ovid briefly describes an imaginary "golden age", which he brings to an end after a mere thirty lines with the thrusting of Saturn into Limbo by "Jove unjust" – after which men misbehave to the best of their ability. Jove attempts to do something about this by flooding the world and drowning everyone except Deucalion and his wife – but the gods then get up to no good themselves, with Apollo chasing Daphne, and Jove (quickly forgetting his indignation) transforming Io into a white cow so as to conceal her from the jealous Juno... In other versions of how the world began, Saturn's son, having seized power from his father, at once set about consolidating it – in ways not unfamiliar to later despots and politicos great and small. For example, Niccolò Machiavelli, in* The Prince *(1513) – taking it for granted that "The wish to acquire more is admittedly a very natural and common thing, and when men succeed in this they are always praised rather than condemned" – says of rulers in* *general, "It is far better to be feared than loved if you cannot be both" since "the bond of love is one which men, wretched creatures that they are, break when it is to their advantage to do so; but fear is strengthened by a dread of punishment which is always effective." And so "when he seizes a state the new ruler ought to determine all the injuries that he will need to inflict" and inflict them with the utmost cruelty. According to Machiavellian statecraft, this constitutes "cruelty used well". But "cruelty badly used is that which, although infrequent to start with, as time goes on, rather than disappearing, grows in intensity". The new ruler is then hated more than feared and "cannot possibly stay in power"... Although myths of the sort adapted in the following Petrarchan – and also Shakespearean – sonnets were often painted during the 15th and 16th centuries in Italy, the artists were paid by those in power. Their cruelty therefore tends to disappear into representations better suited to the public or private chambers of wealthy patrons eager for the respectability which the fine arts as well as the theories of humanism helped to confer on the great shift in moral values from the world of Giotto and St Francis, say, to that of the princes and merchants of the Renaissance with their ever-growing "wish to acquire more":*

i

To start with, Jove pursued his proud twin-sister
Juno, who only yielded to his charms
When the bedraggled dove she'd rescued kissed her –
And forced its way between her legs and arms.

His mother Rhea knew that, if Jove married,
Women were bitched. He raged. She hissed – and grew
Into a snake to scare him. Which miscarried:
Her son out-snaked her snake; and forced her too.

Some say that Venus was Jove's foam-born daughter
(Her mother's parents were the Air and Earth):
Jove watched her perfect body rise from the water,

And rose as well. Thus out of his full horn
Poured gods and men. And Venus soon gave birth
To the god whose bolts caused billions to be born.

ii

Acrisius, Danae's father, should have begged
Great Jove for mercy, rather than have locked
His only daughter – moon-pale, blonde, long-legged –
In a tower of brass. But God is not mocked.

So, rising to the challenge, macho Jove,
Ejaculating sun-light, showered like gold,
Or like a fountain, into his dry love:
Oh, he was more than she could hope to hold!

She'd want no other lover after that.
Their son would lop Medusa's snake-haired head,
And save Andromeda. Jove's lust begat

Blessings on all predestined to enjoy him.
The wimp her father, though, deserved to be dead:
Who better than his grandson to destroy him?

iii

Jove's favourite was the pretty Trojan boy
Who fetched his nectar: honey-skinned, well-hung,
Ganymede blushed like a girl. No human toy,
He'd sulk and fidget. Jove preferred them young.

Juno was jealous, and/or envious. He
Was sure she fancied sexy G. as well.
Hebe, his ex-cup-bearer, chafed. But she
Was Juno's tattling pet. And boys don't tell.

King Tros, his father, cried. The girls all loved him.
As terrified as a child, he'd burst into tears
And pissed himself when Jove the Eagle removed him
From chasing pig-tails, horny beyond his years…

So Jove sent horses and a golden vine
Of Vulcan's. But Tros smashed it. Pearls before swine.

iv

Juno would sometimes groan, "Oh god, you *bull!*"
Which set him thinking. Soon he proudly trotted
Up to Europa, where she walked, arms full
Of flowers, along the sands. They played; he plotted –

Demure and little, with horns as soft as wax –
To lure her off to Crete, where they'd have fun…
And made, for years, the beast with two humped backs.
Lewd girl/boy-humping Minos was their son.

Years later, Pasiphae groaned, "You son of a – *bull?*"
Which set her thinking. Neptune's lightly trod
The waves. Sly Daedalus helped. She felt so full
She thought she'd split, and shrieked, "Oh bull, you *god!* –"

So one bull led to another – bearing fruit
From Jove to man-made, roaring, man-eating brute.

v

The swan great Jove had entered in his need
Flattened and raped the girl. Later, he watched
Her – grunting – bear huge eggs. More blood would bleed –
More guts be split – than Leda's, when they hatched.

Jove claimed Tyndareus had inseminated
Her womb already. Helen was Jove's, of course,
But not sour Clytemnaestra. Pollux – fated
To star among the Immortals by the force

Of his straight right, left hook, and upper-cut –
Invented the Spartan war-dance. Victorious, he
Loved bellicose bards and music. But,

As for that loser Castor, who'd dare claim
That he was Jove's?… His mother? Ah, but she,
After Jove trod her, never spoke again.

4 HEINRICH HEINE: TWO POEMS ON THE HISTORY OF RELIGION

i

Almansor

Heine's Almansor *takes place in and around Córdoba in Andalusia, some time after about 1530... When Granada fell to the Christians in 1492, the mosque at Córdoba was the largest in the Western world – too big (and perhaps too impressive) to demolish. The erection of the present cathedral in the midst of the mosque itself was begun in 1523, as a sign of Christian supremacy. In 1825, not long before his poem was published, Heine, who was born a Jew, was baptized as a Protestant Christian, and Almansor's apostacy is presumably related to his own. Heine changed religion for purely practical reasons (Jews had limited rights in nineteenth-century Germany), and he rather fancied it didn't matter. But it seems to have rankled for the rest of his life.*

(i)

Córdoba's immense cathedral
Stands on thirteen hundred columns:
Under that almighty dome you
Either feel oppressed or solemn...

Verses out of the Koran
Twine like plants in Arabic
Down its mihrab's walls and pillars –
Flowers for pious souls to pick.

Moorish kings once raised these arches
As a mosque to Allah's glory.
But the times have changed. Who lords it
Here is now another story.

Melancholy bells now toll,
Calling Christians from the tower

Where the imam called the Moslems
When the Moslems were in power.

Where the faithful sang the Prophet's
Words and wisdom, chanting prayers,
Tonsured priests now raise their blander
Host from further up the stairs.

And they twist and twirl in front of
Gaudy dolls and holy relics,
And there's smoke and bells and bleating,
And their big dumb candles flicker.

Silent in that huge cathedral
Stands Almansor ben Abdullah,
And observes the many columns –
But no mufti and no mullah.

"Oh, you pillars, once so holy,
Built to march in Allah's praise,
Now you serve our Christian masters'
Hated and unholy ways!

"Moving with the times, your un-moved
Patience helps you bear their cross.
Weaker vessels should be able
Likewise to contain their loss!"

Over the cathedral font,
Thus Almansor ben Abdullah
Primly bends his proud neck, hoping
Soon his life will be cheerfuller.

(ii)

Hastily he leaves the building,
Racing off on his black mare;
In his cap a cocky feather
Braves the blast which dries his hair.

On the way to Alcolea,
By the blue Guadalquivir,
Where the almond blossom whitens
And the orange scents the air,

Like a Christian knight, he gaily
Hunts and whistles, laughs and sings,
And the birds join in, descanting
On the river's mutterings.

On a hill near Alcolea
Stands the castle. Donna Clara
Smiles to think the duke her father
Is off fighting in Navarra.

And Almansor, from a distance,
Hears the drums and trumpets braying;
Sees beneath the trees' dark arches
Flashing lights, musicians playing.

And a dozen ladies dancing
With a dozen knights, all dressed
Up to kill. But, freshly christened,
Don Almansor danced the best.

Treading air, he whirled and flirted
Like Don Juan round the hall;
Knowing how to tease and flatter
Twelve young girls, he pleased them all:

Kissing Isabella's fingers
Lightly, on he lightly danced;
Shyly flirts with shy Elvira,
Eyeing her as if entranced;

With a laugh, asks Leonora
Is he better-dressed today?
Making sure his cloak's embroidered
Golden cross is on display;

Tells each one how much he loves her –
And, to stop them taking fright,
Swears "– as true as I'm a Christian"
Thirty times at least that night.

(iii)

In the hall at Alcolea
All their revels now are ended.
Shadows gather. One last couple
Sit in darkness, unattended,

Donna Clara and Almansor,
Left alone beneath the glimmer
Shed by one last lonely candle,
Which makes solid bodies shimmer…

Clara, shimmering in her armchair,
Holds Almansor's sleepy head,
Which he lays on her sweet knees.
He's so tired he feels half-dead.

Pensively, she pours an attar
Of red roses from a golden
Bottle on his dark-brown hair,
Till his heart-felt sighs embolden

Her to kiss him – press the softness
Of her red lips, pensively,
To his dark, rose-scented curls;
But he frowns so darkly she

Weeps hot tears from her bright eyes,
Pensively, and lets them fall
On Almansor's oily hair,
Till his twitching lips appal

Her red lips, as now he dreams –
Head bowed, weeping, back at home

In among a crowd of voices
Under that almighty dome

Where, in Córdoba, the columns,
Muttering darkly, seem to say
They can't stand it any longer!
Tremors shake the walls – and they

Totter, crack, and start to tumble.
Priests and people blanch and simper.
With a crash the dome collapses
And their gods cry out and whimper.

ii

Princess Sabbath

"You called me dog…" – Shylock,
The Merchant of Venice, I.iii.123

The relationship of Heine's poetry to the social and political history of his time was virtually always confrontational – whether directly and specifically, as in The Slave-Ship *and much of* Germany. A Winter's Tale *(see* Then and Now – Words in the Dark*), or more obliquely, as in* Almansor *and* Princess Sabbath. *Whichever approach he took, though, Heine had the gift of grasping the permanently relevant amid the turbulence of the 'Age of Revolution' – as Eric Hobsbawm called the period from 1789 to 1848 – so that what he wrote still matters, and not only as poetry. As the concluding section of the last full-length volume of poems that he published,* Romanzero *(1851), Heine – always a thoughtful arranger of his work – chose three long and complex pieces on Jewish themes, which he entitled* Hebräische Melodien. *Heine's biographer, J.L. Sammons, comments, "The first and most compact of them is…'Prinzessin Sabbath', which with distanced and ironic sympathy captures the transformation of the poor, servile workaday Jew into a prince on the Sabbath" (Heinrich Heine: A Modern Biography, 1979). But the poem (as often with Heine) is not easy to pin down, and Peter Branscombe (in his 'Introduction' to* Heine: Selected Verse, *1967) describes it as "perhaps the most beautiful of Heine's poetic tributes to the* *religion of his fathers…". Branscombe goes on to say that "the tone of the poem is predominantly one of nostalgia, of a quiet exultation which makes life for all its sufferings worth living". No doubt Heine gets it both ways. Moreover, in the context of nineteenth century anti-Semitism – and with the benefit of hindsight – the disenchanted, as well as enchanted, irony with which Heine invests his subject appears clear-sighted to the point of prophetic. In* The Destruction of the European Jews *(1985), Raul Hilberg describes the sort of isolation or expulsion which the poem adumbrates (ranging in the real world from the barring of Jews from certain professions to ghettoization to enforced emigration) as the second anti-Jewish policy in European history, the first having been conversion to Christianity. Heine himself had endured both and, if he had lived a century later, might have experienced the third, which was annihilation:*

> Sometimes in Arabian folk-tales
> There's a prince who – though enchanted –
> In his handsome human form
> Gets to woo the girl he wanted;
>
> And a king's son nobly swaggers,
> Back from being a hairy brute,
> Dressed in rich and brilliant garments,
> Playing love-songs on the flute.
>
> But the magic respite passes,
> And His Royal Highness stands
> Once again a shaggy monster
> With the flute in his huge hands…
>
> Long ago a witch's Evil
> Eye turned one prince, Israel,
> Into a stray dog – although he
> Keeps on trying to break the spell.
>
> All week long, with doggy thoughts,
> Eating refuse, sniffing turds,
> Through the streets he runs, enduring
> Urchins' stones and, worse, their words.

But at dusk on Friday evening
Suddenly the spell grows weaker,
And the dog's a man again –
Princely lover, earnest seeker

After truth, with thoughts and feelings,
And his human head held high,
Entering then the king his father's
Doorway, dressed-up festively,

Washed and brushed, and greeting proudly
Those familiar halls: "Once more,
Jacob's tents, I kiss the sacred
Door-posts of your sacred doors!"

Through the house mysterious whispers
Weave the history of the Word:
Awesomely, amid the silence,
Breathes the house's unseen Lord.

Silence! Only the Lord's steward
(*Vulgo* synagogue attendant)
Hops about there, lighting lamps:
Some are standing, others pendant,

All convey religious solace,
Shining, gleaming, deep in shade,
While the candles proudly flicker
On the almemor's balustrade.

By the shrine in which the Torah
Rests, and which is decorated
With a costly silken cover,
Gilded, jewelled, illuminated,

Stands the cantor, at his prayer-desk –
A coquettish little man,
Who adjusts his smart black coat as
Noticeably as he can.

Showing off his soft white hands, he
Fingers first his neck and then,
Index-finger to his forehead,
Places thumb to throat again

In a curious gesture, humming
Quietly to himself, until
Lecho Daudi Likras Kalle!
Rings out loud and clear to fill

The entire hall with jubilation –
"Come, beloved, to the place
Where thy waiting bride unveils
For thine eyes her timid face."

This high-minded song was penned by
Don Jehuda ben Halevy,
Who – a troubador – was one of
The most famous sons of Levi.

In his song is celebrated
Israel's marriage to the peerless
Princess Sabbath, still and silent,
And as flawless as a pearl is,

Or a flower of perfect beauty –
Lovelier, for example, than
That great Queen of Sheba, brightest
Confidante of Solomon,

Who, blue-stockinged Ethiopian,
With her brilliant quips and/or
Cunning riddles, set to dazzle,
Soon became a crashing bore,

While the Princess, as the very
Personification of
Peace and quiet, detests all showy
Intellectual push and shove,

Not to mention all excited
Loudness, stamping or declaiming
Grandly, storming in with hair
Wind-blown and in need of combing.

And she covers, with a bonnet,
Her own chastely plaited tresses,
Blooming like a slender myrtle,
With gazelle-like eyes and lashes,

Though she lets her princeling do
Anything but smoke – would say
"Darling! Smoking is a no-no
On the holy sabbath day –

But, instead, today at lunch-time
You'll find steaming on the table
Heavenly schalet. And you may
Eat as much as you are able."

Schalet, schöner Götterfunken,
Tochter aus Elysium!
That's how Schiller's anthem would have
Sounded if he'd tasted some.

Heavenly schalet is the food
Which our dear Lord God himself
Once showed Moses where to gather
On Mount Sinai's topmost shelf,

Where He wrote the Ten Commandments
And the Law, as in His book,
Teaching Moses in the storm-cloud
How to judge and what to cook.

Schalet is the Lord our God's
Genuine ambrosia –
Blissful fruit of Paradise –
And so far beyond compare

That the ambrosia of those spurious
Heathen gods of ancient Greece
Seems like devils' excrement:
Weren't they devils in disguise?

Which is why, when eating schalet,
Israel's princely eyes start gleaming.
He unbuttons his best waistcoat
And intones, as if day-dreaming,

"Once again I hear the Jordan
Streaming and the rumbling springs
Of the palm-filled vale at Bethel,
Camels, distant ting-a-lings

Rung by herdsmen's fat bell-wethers
As they lead their lambs and sheep
Evenings down Mount Gileath's slopes to
Fields where they can safely sleep…"

But the Sabbath will be over
Soon. As if on shadow legs,
Like a dog, the hour comes running –
Israel's courage sighs and sags,

As he feels its mocking, ice-cold
Eyes transfix his heart of hearts.
And a shudder runs right through him
Now, in case the dog-change starts,

Till the princess kindly hands him
Her nard-box of solid gold.
Slowly he inhales it, hoping
That its airy charm will hold…

Quickly the sad princess pours him
One last goblet. Once again,
He as quickly drains it. Only
A few drops of wine remain.

These he sprinkles on the table
In the flickering candle-light.
Dunks the candle in the puddle,
Where it sputters and goes out.

5 SELF-PORTRAIT AS A WHITE-COLLAR WORKER (4) – AFTERWORDS

i

Working for the Enemy

No work on "our side" meant that he – "like a spy" –
Felt forced to slave for umpteen years on "theirs":
For the sake of his art, he claimed – to leave it free
Of markets, fashions, cliques, to do or be
Whatever it needed. At last, the job and its cares
Silenced him. Left him puzzling over why.

He thought he'd grown, perhaps, to believe his lies:
At first we act them, then we act on them.
Once an escape from the gold-and-ivory tower,
"Useful experience" had gradually assumed more power
Over his heart and mind – by guilt and shame
As well as muddied, muddled compromise –

Than he'd ever expected. Though he held that art
Can swallow any subject – even the pride
Of the wounded artist – he knew as well that he ought
To have left that place where bodies and souls are bought,
Whose ways are all dead ends, where he might have died –
Of stomach cancer, say, or a stricken heart –

But, dully, suffered on. Self-punishment
Takes many forms. A more or less settled gloom
Grew slowly thicker, rarely now relieved
By doing things in which he still believed –
By looking forward to less fear, less boredom –
Or saying, for instance, what he really meant.

Disgusted, insecure, self-alienated,
Yet still condoning corporate power and greed,
He also told himself such sacrifice –

Which only went to show how little choice
We really have – was needed if the needs
Of his family were to be accommodated…

And so he managed. While others managed the world.
But art needs deep slow truth, the spiralling peace
Beyond all understanding. Not, of course,
As therapy, or some hermeneutic pause
In the race for gold. Or even here. But at least
As an end – in view or not – whereto we're swirled

Like eddies in a stream. We write to live;
He lived to try and find the time to write:
"What poets need above all things is luck! –
Plus native wit, perhaps, or witless pluck –
To help them through this fight that's not their fight,
This give-and-take that's only *take* not *give*…"

And yet, when he retired, he wished he'd done
Something to try and curb the booming harm
To human nature and/or the Nature we share –
Their actual earth and water, fire and air –
Instead of (in secret) sounding a quiet alarm
In ever fewer words. The enemy won.

ii

Stephanskirchen (1)

*"The moment that his face I see,
I know the man that must hear me."*
                    Coleridge, ***The Ancient Mariner***

Although he thought he'd get what he deserved –
An unfulfilled, dull, unfulfilling life –
"The observer must be more than the observed,"
Observed his undefeated, German wife…

*

Today, they were revisiting the church
Of a tiny village – *Wirtshaus*, school, two farms –
Which an Allied bomber (lost perhaps) in search
Of other targets, riding an Alpine storm,

Hit and destroyed one black and blinding night
In mid-November, 1944:
Re-built on its green hill, and gleaming white
In the Easter sun, the church outlives the war…

Below it, the German landscape Primo Levi
Found "rich and civilized" – vast fields, thick forests,
Geraniums on house-fronts – flourished under the heavy
Aura of the history sun and church forget.

Their last time here – an outing with the firm
The previous summer – an eighty-year-old man,
Or so he claimed, addressed them in a firm
And interested voice, as they began

To read – as visitors will – the fading names
And ages of the local dead, whose graves
He tended – simple epitaphs, brief rhymes,
German for *Rest in Peace* or *Jesus saves*:

"It's nice up here," he'd grinned. "But not down there" –
Where wilting flowers and wreaths half-hid a mound:
"Bavaria's known for *Föhn* – blue skies – clear air –
But you don't get much of that beneath the ground…

Look at this family here, for instance." They'd
Paused by a plain black stone, commemorating
Four fallen sons. Beside them their parents lay –
Rosa and Franz – who'd died a short time later.

One son lived on for thirty years and more.
"Their youngest was my schoolfriend. Here's our teacher.

At over seventy, he taught right through the war.
His daughter was a very pretty creature.

But after I'd gone missing, presumed dead,
She married my best friend. Left in the lurch,
I married hers." And, with a laugh, he'd led
Them both inside the perfectly restored church –

An early Gothic structure with baroque
Statues and gaily painted ornamentation
Which also displayed, no larger than a plaque,
Evidence of almost literal decimation:

Thirty-three *Sterbebilder*, in a frame,
Of Hemhof's war-dead – some no more than boys,
Others not even wearing uniform,
A Nazi or two: "*God gives and God destroys…*"

He'd jabbed a grubby finger: "That one's me.
I turned up later, long after the war
Was over. So they left me. As you can see,
The English dropped in on us once before":

A photo of the church minus its spire
And half its nave. Old Rumpelstiltskin smiled
With teeth askew: "Well, no hard feelings. The fire
That stormy night, though, could be seen for miles.

Or so they say. I was a long way east
Of here by then. And didn't see a thing…
The work's my pastime. Tiring now. At least
Our modern bells aren't difficult to ring" –

And he'd flicked a switch to show them what he meant…
Now, in the unnaturally hot Easter sun,
The six-year winter of war's discontent
Was hard to imagine – and had been so then.

Facing the cemetery, across the lane,
Under an ancient wooden barn's wide eaves,
Six beehives, as in Brueghel, still looked down,
Long empty of their bees, baking beneath

The dazzling, deep-blue sky. The church and woods
And *Wirtshaus* slept in their old Sunday silence…
"There's nothing like the sun – until you're dead,"
He'd grinned again, and gone about his business.

*

Mid-day. And not a sound on either farm.
They entered the old *Wirtshaus* with its thick
Walls and small windows – cool in summer, warm
In winter. Painted eggs, to 'peck' and crack,

Filled nest-like baskets on each table-mat.
The *Wirt*, a former colleague's uncle, brought
Beer and fresh *Bretzeln*. Three or four locals sat
Drinking around their *Stammtisch*, or sunk in thought.

"Last summer," he asked his wife, "do you remember
The 'modern' bells, while the others strolled ahead? –
Our very own Tiresias telling the number
Of the ancient parish church's young war-dead?" –

"Then, after dinner, when he hobbled in,
You joined him – "
                    "Having ordered *zwei Maß Bier* – "
"While the others talked dull shop."
                                    "Ah, well, you win
Some and you lose some. As he said. In here.

Behind you, in that corner, on His cross,
He praised the Son of Man, who lost *and* won,
Like war-torn Germany – which healed its loss
By spinning gold from straw… Well, I've begun

Trying to remember what he said – thought – saw –
And making notes for a long poem on why
So *many* goose-stepped off to Hitler's war…
I went to work – but not, I hope, to die!

He laughed when I said that. He himself knew
He wouldn't die. He'd volunteered before
Being press-ganged by the *Waffen-SS*, who
Did Hitler's dirty work. When asked what for,

He seemed less certain: 'Everyone went who could…
Not only because they had to. Many believed
Their solemn duty was to fight for the good
Of *Reich – Volk – Führer…*' Some were less deceived,

Perhaps. But Nazism somehow left you no words
To think with… He – was young and tired of home,
Of farm-work – enclosed by mountains, endless woods –
Of waiting for some change, for things to come…

So why not go, he'd thought – *and* make *things change!*
No one could ever have imagined how
Bad it would get. – *Over that mountain-range*
Life must be better… He knew better now.

As for the crassest fascists, those in thrall
To Hitler's crazed illusions, 'We Germans love
To lead and be led, you know. And *Over all*
Was *Deutschland, Deutschland*' – led from the front and above,

In bold defiance of the League of Nations,
The *Amis* and the Brits, the French and Poles,
Who'd revelled in the Reich's humiliation,
The injury and the insult of Versailles,

With words – words – words that drove ecstatic crowds
Like herds to roar and bellow, shed hot tears,
Rage, groan, laugh, hiss as one – all armed, all proud
To lose their individual minds and fears –

By someone who, he'd thought, was hardly sane
To start with, and in time became unfit
To lead at all. But they slaughtered and were slain,
Their most inviolable slogan being *Macht mit!* –

First mobbed, then murdered (scapegoat-like) the Jews,
Their 'enemy within', for plotting what
Would further *them*. The Slump was front-page news;
But storm-troopers got good boots, and shirts, and hats.

The Jews were *different* – foreign – self-employed –
Agreed / refused you credit – paid your employer:
'The socialism of idiots' marched to destroy
Their 'threat' to international German power.

The SS motto's counter-threat – '*My Honour
Is* total and unquestioning *Loyalty*' –
Later assigned crack squads the role of goner:
Theirs was to do, theirs not to reason why – "

"He didn't say that."
                      "No. But, towards the end,
The Nazi faithful, fearing the war was lost,
Ran senseless risks. He'd seen whole units sent
To do and die, and not to count the cost –

Youthful fanatics pledge to shoot one another,
Or else themselves, before they'd ever surrender.
And dares were rife. Old rivals dared each other,
Outfacing their own fears, to kill – rape – plunder…

The *Wehrmacht's* last-ditch orders were to destroy
Revolt or armed resistance, where they unearthed it,
'With the utmost ruthless harshness' – to deploy
Round-ups, reprisals, terror to deter it:

Mercy or pity was mere Christian weakness.
Not that he'd ever held such heathen views;
But for some the faith of Jesus was a sickness

To sap the strong – hatched by (who else?) the Jews.

Others, though, blamed the Jews for killing Jesus.
Every loud weakling found some cause to hate them:
Unfairly clever, powerful, rich as Croesus…
Perverts and numbskulls strove to exterminate them…

Not being a coward, he'd had no need to prove
His manhood by inhuman, sick excesses.
Homesick and sex-starved and, worse, starved of love,
They fought, and dreamt of *Lilli Marleen's* caresses.

But you might as well waste food or ammunition
As spill your beans in war. Not soft but hard
Options meant *'Pleasure generates submission'*:
The sentimental rapist's off his guard –

And, *post coitum*, swings from sad to mad…
– I elaborate again. But, veteran or callow
Sixteen-year-old, true troopers had to be led.
Where wise or crack-brained shepherds go, herds follow…"

– " *'Goats to the left and sheep to the right.'* "
                                       " *'They're split*
Without much bother…' But 'our surest defence
Is something that can't be feigned – faked – imitated –
Or even shared' – and yet makes (common) sense.

Whereas the force and lures we all deploy
To get what we've been schooled – drilled – fooled to desire
Still now, with quiet legality, destroy
Our souls in the great industrial / military fire…

Like war, like work. Ambition – slogans – fads –
Or (as Bavarians say) if you drive a sow
Up the main village street, for good or bad,
Every fool tries to ride her. Then, as now,

It struck and troubled, strikes and troubles me

How nations vie like firms – how firms deploy
Their work-force like a peace-time army. We
Are briefed who to compete with, who to destroy –

Receive our orders, which we leap to obey,
Or more or less adjust to suit ourselves,
Proud of our mission, treating perks and pay
As signs of status, which all work involves…

At such a time as that, in such a place,
How many went to war in much the same
Bad faith as we to work at such as this:
Because we've learned that '*History is to blame*'?

It seems, at least, that governments, like boards,
Direct or try to choose their people's fate – "
"You chose retirement."
                              "In less retiring words,
Those killed in friendly fire left it too late!

They soldiered on. Most businessmen find peace
To their advantage. But unrestricted growth
Struggles for unrestricted means – for space
In which to grow. War is the blinding truth

Which follows as the night follows the day
When phoney friends expire. The business mind
In-forms us, pouring oil on the barbed-wire way
Down which the war-like blind then race the blind…

The paths of glory lead we all know where.
Big / bigger / biggest business names the game,
And no one can tell which future horrors war
Hauls in its wake but *More (and more) of the same.*

While 'business as usual' booms / busts / booms, though, we –
As individuals – can, we know, survive
Either by emigrating inwardly – "

"By compromising?"
                      "Or, defiantly alive –

As Rumpelstiltskin knew he wouldn't die –
By exploiting what we find. He flowed with the flow:
By raising no resistance to today
Fought on – and puts the past behind him now…

Others he'd known who, half in love with pain,
Waiting for orders, trained to hear and obey –
Too passive, with too little will of their own –
Soon died, losing themselves, or lost their way.

While many who went because they'd always done
As they were told – or (with no real idea
Of why their brothers, neighbours, friends had gone)
Because so many that they knew were there –

Soon died as well. In war you had to *fight*
Not just the enemy but senseless orders,
Lack of equipment, boots, food: every sort
Of lousy luck – foul weather – ill-mapped borders –

And, towards the end, the total madness of
(As no one dared say then) the Berlin bunker,
Whose Nordic *Götterdämmerung* – in love
With Death itself – dragging the whole world under,

Went under first. Under the circumstances,
Bigots who'd joined the *Heer* convinced they ought
To do their German duty lost their senses
As *Deutschland, Deutschland* lost all sane support…

Most genuine fascists weren't tough farmers' sons,
Or Catholics like himself, but middle-class
Embittered townees, strapped, hard-done-by since
The Kaiser's 'place in the sun' had risen and passed.

At home, before he'd left, more than a few

Had laughed at Hitler. Not that there was much
That farmers, hop-growers, fishermen could *do*
Or even say. Apart from wait and watch…

Shop-keepers, teachers, lawyers, white-collar workers
Of every kind had lost their lives or their nerve.
By avoiding heroes, burn-outs, drunks, berserkers
And cowards, he'd hoped and managed to survive…"

– "Where I grew up, the eldest son of three,
On hearing (the story went) his wounded brother
Had died in Warsaw when the Infirmary
Came under fire, had horrified his father

By angrily hanging Hitler's official portrait –
Among the other rats and bugs, he said –
Behind the pigsty, in the outside toilet.
The father, swearing they'd all end up dead,

Lugged it back in. Their youngest, home on leave,
Had tried to crush one foot with the big stone
For pressing kraut. Each time it dropped he'd move
The foot away. At last, they cracked a bone,

But only three months later he was sent
With other bumpkins less than fighting keen
On Hitler's war, to man the Russian front.
He got to Moscow – and was never seen

Again. His friend who'd helped him with the stone
Had long been badly wounded. Soon to die,
He transported his whole family from bombed Köln:
More food, no air-raids, milk, a star-filled sky…

He also had two children (one was me)
With different women. Thus his last two years
Passed quietly. He emigrated inwardly.
The village was like this one."
                                – "Though, it appears

When Rumpelstiltskin walked back out of the war
Between the woodland lakes along the track
Or *Römerweg* from Seebruck, the church looked more
Like Dresden or Berlin. Relieved to be back,

He'd swum in Hartsee, then in Kesselsee,
At his old bathing places. Nothing had changed.
Emerging from the wood to see blue sky
But no spire above the full-grown maize felt strange –

Though no one, he'd found, was hurt. He'd helped rebuild
Their bit of history. Everyone helped who could.
Already gummed and framed, his *Sterbebild*
Was left among the well and truly dead.

They wanted peace, not war, to have the last word,
He claimed, and sank that block of stone in the earth
To say it: 'GIVE US PEACE IN OUR TIME, O LORD'
It pleads with empty heaven. For what *that's* worth."

– "Perhaps such prayers aren't only a waste of breath,
If the speaker *hears* them…"
                                   "Over their stone the plain
Black cross with 'IN THE MIDST OF LIFE IS DEATH'
Across its wings resembles an aeroplane

Ascending the church's blank, white Eastern wall…
His cheerful fortitude was what impressed me –
His stoical detachment. After all,
With nothing like war's crazed ordeal to test me,

I'd say I managed nothing like as well."
– "You had more choices. But did he have none?
The Nazis' words and deeds were there for all
To hear and see… What if he hadn't gone?"

– "Dachau?"
               "And yet Ernst Jandl, for example,
Called up in Vienna after leaving school,

Defected at the front. Nothing was simple,
But only Nazi thugs or rogues or fools,

Surely, kept fighting? From very early on,
Hitler made public and political use
Of violence – SA terror – such that no one
Could miss it. And so what was *his* excuse

For turning a blind eye?"
                         "He never said
A lot about it."
                "Nor about where he'd been
Either before or after he was 'dead'.
Or what he'd done and not done – must have seen…"

*

They paid the *Wirt*, who poured them schnapps – "On the house!" –
And wished them *Frohe Ostern*, asking after
His nephew, other colleagues, and the price
Of beer in England. With greetings and friendly laughter,

They took their leave and, alarmed to find outside
The gathering clouds of an April thunderstorm,
Cycled off quickly down the Roman road
To Gstadt – away from war's forgotten alarms.

   iii

   after jandl

description of a life
(i.m. dietrich burkhard)

he has talent
the professor said to my mother.

he's very talented
my mother said to my father.
i have talent, the professor said to my mother
i said to my friend.

my father had a long life.
my father had hardly any white hair left.
my mother stopped plucking her white hair out hair by hair.
women don't want to develop a bald patch.
my father had so much time.
i won't be renewing
our acquaintance.

my name was dietrich.
at fifteen i wrote a tango.
i played the tango for my professor
and the professor said: i'll take care of
your further training and development,
and my mother said to my father
they'll take care of his training.

in 1926 i received my residence permit.
on it is written: 1926 to . . . .
19 in print and 26 in green ink
to the four printed dots;
the authorities were thinking of the third thousand years.
the authorities think a long time in advance.

my name was dietrich.
i had a talent for useless things.
in 1926 i received my residence permit.
i left primary school when i was nine.
at fifteen i wrote a tango.
at seventeen i passed my exams.
since 1944 i write the number 18
on official forms in the space for my age…

he has talent
the professor said to my mother.

he's very talented
my mother said to my father.
he should apply for something
my father said.
but i didn't apply for anything.

so they made me wear a grey jacket
and sat at home and wrote picture postcards
and cut their nails every day.
we'll take care of his training
the sergeant said to my mother,
and took the stalk of grass from between his teeth;
give that to his professor and tell him
it's not a question of talent, only of training.

my name was dietrich.
from 1926 to 1944.
now i don't have a name any longer.
from day to day there's less of me
and the enormous diggers of death
which for some time now
have quaked across the earth again
accelerate the process
of my further development.

(lebensbeschreibung from *Dingfest)*

what they can do to you

what they could do to you?
they could rip out your tongue.
you were never much of a speaker.
they could gouge out your eyes.
haven't you seen enough yet?
deprive you of your manhood.
you were never much use as a man.
dislocate your fingers.

you shouldn't pick your nose in any case.
hack off your feet.
at your age you ought to sit more.
torture you till you go mad.
everyone thinks you're crazy anyway.

> *(was sie dir tun können* from *Dingfest)*

tell us about the war, dad
tell us how you signed on, dad
tell us how you shot 'em, dad
tell us how you were wounded, dad
tell us how you were killed, dad
tell us about the war, dad

> *(vater komm erzähl vom krieg* from *Dingfest)*

manner of speaking

i'll
break
you
yet
you
get

fatherbendmerather

> *(redensart* from *Sprechblasen)*

cromwell

the horizon says goodnight
and chops off heads like trees
hardly have they said amen

before they're spiked on their dreams

mrs cromwell comes and crows till they wake
grafts each head to a neck
paints cuckold blood on the stitches
soon something stirs in the commonwealth

(cromwell from *Dingfest)*

16 years

thickthdeen years
thentral thdayshun
thickthdeen years
what'th hegoin
what'th hegoin
to do
thentral thdayshun
thickthdeen years
what'th hegoin
what'th hegoin
the lad
what'th hegoin
to do
what'th hegoin
what'th hegoin
to do
thickthdeen years
thentral thdayshun
what'th hegoin
to do
the lad
with hith
thickthdeen years

(16 jahr from *Laut and Luise)*

she can cook

lots of dogs old women girlsheads and other needs or wishes
all get thrown into the one bucket
when she walks through the streets.
like a housewife home from market she empties on the kitchen table
kraut radishes fruit and prawns out of her shoppingbag
rolls the old women lots of dogs and the girlsheads
like raisins nuts and lemonpeel
in the pastry of her needs
or wishes – opens herself and is the oven
which does the baking. she can cook.

(sie kann kochen from *Dingfest)*

in the deli

could you give me some maymeadow conserve, please,
fairly high up but not so steep
that you can't sit down on it.
well, then perhaps a snowy slope, deepfrozen,
containing no skiers, and a nice firtree
hung with snow, if you happen to have one.

then what about – hares, i see you've hung some hares.
two or three will do. and of course a hunter.
where do you hang your hunters?

(im delikatessen laden from *Dingfest)*

surfacetranslation (1)

du bist wie eine blume
so hold und schön und rein
ich schau dich an und wehmut
schleicht mir ins herz hinein.

mir ist als ob ich die hände
aufs haupt dir legen sollt
betend dass gott dich erhalte
so rein und schön und holt.

                (heinrich heine)

do pissed v. iron a bloomer
so halt & sean & ryan
hicks how dick ann away mute
sh liked mere inns hurts he nine.

mere hissed al sob hick the end a
ow/eff sow/put deer lay gun salt
bait end ass got dicker halter
so ryan & sean & halt.

           (*oberflächenübersetzung* from *Sprechblasen*)

wht y cn d wtht vwls

kss
fck
lck
sck
pss
sht

                (*ohne vocale* from *Der künstliche Baum*)

rilke, rhymeless

rilke
he said

then he said
gherkin

softly then
cloud

> *(rilke reimlos* from *gedichter)*

rilke's weight

is to be taken
off rilke's mind

thus, rough-and-ready, the earth
brings up her son

> *(rilke's gewicht* from *gedichter)*

surfacetranslation (2) : feel

... o	... o
sophie	sophy
so	so
solo	solo
sophie	sophy
solo	solo
so	so
o	o
so	so
solo	solo

sophie	sophy
o	o
so	so
viel	feel
vieh	fee
sophie	sophy
o	o
so	so
solo	solo
sophie	sophy
o	o
so	so
viel	feel
sophie	sophy
[etcetera]	[ate, set her hair]
o	o
sophie	sophy
so	so
viel	feel
o	o
sophie	sophy
so	so
viel	feel
o	o
sophie	sophy
so	so
viel	feel
vieh	fee
o	o
sophie	sophy
o	o
so	so
viel	feel
o	o
sophie	sophy
viel	feel
o	o

sophie	sophy
viel	feel
o	o
o	o
sophie	sophy

        (viel from *Laut und Luise*)

sonnet

an a an e an i an o a you
a you an a an e an i an o
a you an a an e an i an o
an a an e an i an o a you

an a an e an i an o a you
a you an a an e an i an o
a you an a an e an i an o
an a an e an i an o a you

an o a you an a an e an i
an i an o a you an a an e
an e an i an o a you an a

an o a you an a an e an i
an i an o a you an a an e
an e an i an o a you an a

        (sonett from *Der künstliche Baum*)

otto's mops

otto's mops flops
otto: on, mops, on
otto's mops hops off

otto: oho oho

otto totes coal
otto totes oats
otto stops
otto: mops mops
otto hopes

otto's mops knocks
otto: come, mops, come
otto's mops comes
otto's mops squats
otto: ogodogod

>	(*ottos mops* from *Der künstliche Baum*)

owls

you owls
yes
i'm owls

yes yes
very owls

you owls too
yes
i'm owls too
very owls
yes yes

but don't want to be owls any more
been owls too long already

yes
with you here
with you here too
i'm not owls any more

i'm not owls any more either
yes yes
yes yes too

but once you've been owls
you're always owls
yes

yes yes

      (eulen from *Laut und Luise)*

fifth now

door open
one out
one in
fourth now

door open
one out
one in
third now

door open
one out
one in
second now

door open
one out
one in
next now

door open
one out

you in
mornin'doctor

(fünfte sein from *Der künstliche Baum)*

judgement

the poems of this man are useless.

to start with
i rubbed them into my bald patch.
to no effect. they failed to make my hair grow.

thereupon
i dabbed them on my spots. but these
grew as big as potatoes in only a day or two.
the doctors were astounded.

thereupon
i cooked a couple.
somewhat mistrustful, i refrained from eating them,
as a result of which my dog died.

thereupon
i used them as contraceptives
and paid for an abortion.

thereupon
i wore one as a monocle
and joined a better club.
the doorman
tripped me as i entered.

thereupon
i pronounced judgement as above.

(urteil from *Dingfest)*

perfection

e
ee
eei
eeio

p
pr
prf
prfc
prfct
prfctn

ep
eepr
eeiprf
eeioprfc
eeioprfct
eeioprfctn

pe
pree
prfeei
prfceeio
prfcteeio
prfctneeio

prfcteneio
prfcetneio
prfectneio
prefctneio
perfctneio

perfctenio
perfcetnio
perfectnio

perfectino
perfection

    (perfektion from *Sprechblasen)*

higher and higher

THE MAN CLIMBS ON THE CHAIR
the man stands on the chair
THE CHAIR CLIMBS ON THE TABLE
the man stands on the chair
the chair stands on the table
THE TABLE CLIMBS ON THE HOUSE
the man stands on the chair
the chair stands on the table
the table stands on the house
THE HOUSE CLIMBS ON THE MOUNTAIN
the man stands on the chair
the chair stands on the table
the table stands on the house
the house stands on the mountain
THE MOUNTAIN CLIMBS ON THE MOON
the man stands on the chair
the chair stands on the table
the table stands on the house
the house stands on the mountain
the mountain stands on the moon
THE MOON CLIMBS ON THE NIGHT
the man stands on the chair
the chair stands on the table
the table stands on the house
the house stands on the mountain
the mountain stands on the moon
the moon stands on the night

    (immer höher from *Der künstliche Baum)*

time flies

      fantastic!
     fanfantastictic
    fanfunfantastictoctic
   funfanfunfantastictoctictoc
  fanfunfanfunfantastictoctictoctic

    (die zeit vergeht from *Sprechblasen)*

antipodes

       a sheet
and under it
       a sheet
and under that
       a sheet
and under that
       a sheet
and under that
       a table
and under that
       a floor
and under that
       a room
and under that
       a cellar
and under that
       an earth
and under that
       a cellar
and under that
       a room
and under that
       a table
and under that

                a sheet
and under that
                a sheet
and under that
                a sheet
and under that
                a sheet

    (antipodes from *Der künstliche Baum)*

long load

some people think
that light and reft
can never be
contused.
          Tub bat's
a thig misfake!

    (lichtung from *Laut und Luise)*

two handsigns

i cross myself
before every church
i cherry myself
before every orchard

how i do the first
all catholics know
how i do the other
i alone

    (zweierlei handzeichen from *Laut und Luise)*

book and nose

it was a book, and again
a book, and another, and another one
and many others; he picked one up,
leafed quickly through it, and then another,
and another one, leafing
and finding nothing, nothing at all
for him.
nothing for him now, till he remembered
dietrich's nose, his blond head
and long thin fingers, which raised
the book, some book, open till it cracked,
to his nose, which then inhaled
its bookish fragrance deeply.
dietrich whose life, before the war
ended, had ended.

(buch und nase from *Der gelbe Hund)*

fallen

he fell, and now
he fell too – he,
often enough, had fallen
on his knee, and scraped
the skin, so that his mother
treated it then
with iodine. But
he fell here sounds so
heavy as if more
must have happened than
a bleeding knee, a burn, a scab
and lastly some pink
now where the scab
has fallen off.

(gefallen from *Der gelbe Hund)*

contents

i have nothing
to make a poem

a whole language
a whole life
a whole mind
a whole memory

i have nothing
to make a poem

> (inhalt from *Der gelbe Hund*)

iv

Death and Brandner Caspar – A True Story
(after Franz von Kobell)

> "But, hark! I'll tell ye of a plot,
> Though dinna ye be speakin' o't"
>   Burns, ***Death and Dr Hornbrook***

In 1871, Franz, Ritter von Kobell published a folk-tale in Bavarian dialect – now well known throughout Bavaria – called Die Gschicht von Brandner-Kasper. *In this tale, an old countryman, Brandner Caspar, is sitting alone in his cottage when Death –* the Boanlkramer *or bone-merchant – enters and tells him it's time to go. But Brandner Caspar gets him drunk and wins twenty more years by cheating at cards. Some time later St Peter discovers that Brandner Caspar is still alive and sends Death to fetch him at once. But Death has given his word: what is he to do?*

In the following adaptation, von Kobell receives a letter from Brandner Caspar's grandson. Later, he rewrites the letter to produce his own version of events:

                                Wiessee, 6th January, 1841

Dear Prof. von Kobell,
                    Many thanks
For your inquiry *re* the *Schwank*,
Or tales told then but since re-told,
Of my notorious grandad. Old,
He took much pride in his reputation
For cunning, cards, and conversation –
And, yes, his bet with Death was the game
Of chance which really made his name…
But let me, since I've got all day
To write – my pupils are away
Visiting their own grandad! – try
To present the past more truthfully.
Locksmith, gunsmith, poacher – *Hail, fellow,
Well met* – old Caspar's fame as a teller
Of *Märchen* led the Brothers Grimm
To jot down three or four from him,
Especially of the gruesome type,
Recounted puffing on his pipe,
Which hid him in a cloud of smoke.
And, then, he loved to hoax or joke –
Which made it harder still to extract
The truth from untruth, fiction from fact…

One fact was, when my dad returned
From fighting Bonaparte, he learned
His dad had died the year before
(That is, in 1804),
Aged eighty. Or had disappeared.
It even seems foul play was feared:
The woods and hills were searched all round,
But Caspar's corpse was never found…
Later, when I was three years old
Or four, my father, Toni, told
Me *Brandner Caspar*, just as though
He were a real-life *Märchen*-hero.
Whereas, in fact, when his wife died

And Toni and Georg were abroad,
Foot-slogging with their regiments,
Alone and grieving, Caspar spent
His evenings, then his afternoons
And mornings, drinking schnapps, till soon
His friends were sure he'd die as well.
My father used the same old still
For making his own *Obstler*. Even
His brothers, my great-uncles, had given
Poor Caspar up for lost. But then
One Sunday he appeared again
At nearby Gindlalm, unsteady
But hobbling unassisted, ready
To astound his *Stammtisch* pals with what
Had *knock-knock-knocked* the previous night
In Albach at his cottage door.
His two wise brothers, Melchior,
A priest in Gmund, and Balthazar,
Who poured them drinks behind the bar,
Being landlord, were among those who
First heard the tale about which you
Were asking, sir, in your good letter.
Toni would have remembered better –
But let's pretend, though he's long dead,
We know what Brandner Caspar said:

He said, "My brothers – neighbours – friends,
Last night, while musing on our ends
And means, a knock at my front-door,
Where no one ever knocks (the more
So since my dear wife Traudl died),
Amazed me. In the woods outside,
Rain crashed through wildly threshing trees:
Who's out and about on nights like these,
I wondered, *far from their own home?*
On my threshold, hunched against the storm,
As white as if he had no blood,
A sort of rag-and-bone-man stood,
A hollow-eyed and skeletal fellow,

Grasping a tattered, smashed umbrella,
In tramp's top hat and ruined suit,
But very black. And, black as soot,
His boots were too worn out and wet
To warm his bony sockless feet.
So cold he was that the streaming rain,
As if bleak March had come again,
Plastered his brolly with freezing snow.
'Either come in,' I said, 'or go
And the Devil take you.' In he jumped
And hopped on my table. My heart pumped
And pounded. Till the Bone-man said
'Caspar, now that your wife is dead,
I hoped you'd welcome me as a friend.'
But, face-to-skull with Everyman's End,
I instantly sat up straight. A cup
Of well-water helped me sober up
Before I replied, with a clearer mind,
'Well, Mr Bones, it's more than kind
Of you to think of me. I'll do
What I can to prepare myself for you…
Is that your teeth I can hear chattering?'
– 'I'm *always* cold,' he clattered: 'Stop nattering.'
'But before,' I begged, 'I meet my doom,
Allow me, at least, to tidy my room.'
He grumbled, 'Why? All right, be *quick!*'
 – 'Five minutes ought to do the trick.
But while you clack your heels, perhaps
You'll take, to warm you, a small schnapps?'
'I'm *never* thirsty,' Death replied.
 – 'Then try a titchy sip.' He tried
A large-ish one, and hit the ceiling.
Luckily, he can't have had much feeling
In his dead head: 'My G-d, what's that?'
He gasped – and quickly hung his hat,
With '*Christe eleison!*', over the Cross
In *Herrgottswinkel*. 'That's my Boss,'
He whispered: 'Anyway, His Son.'
 – 'So, how about another one?'

I poured another, which he swallowed
In a single gulp. The leaps which followed
All round the room brought on a cough
Which might have carried the cougher off,
Had he not been himself the Grim Reaper –
Everyman's brother's undying keeper.
'That's spirits. I'm a spirit!' he
Cackled: 'That's my first joke. Tee-hee.
The bottle's half-empty, I'm half-full:
That's optimism. But why so dull,
My friend? *Prost!* One for your last road!'
– 'Now, hold your horses, Bones. I've vowed
To live at least as long, if you please,
As my father, who popped off in peace
At ninety. Hence my long wry face.
Croak now at seventy?! What a disgrace.'
– 'But, Caspar, you can't live forever!'
'Ninety,' I stickled: 'If you're so clever,
Let's cut the cards. Whoever draws
The Joker wins. The bottle's yours,
In any case.' Death took a slug.
Dear friends and neighbours, I'm no mug
And, dealing by far the larger heap
To pickled Bones, contrived to keep
The Joker up my sleeve. Thus his sting
Was stung by my crafty card-sharping –
Willy nilly – for twenty-odd years.
His eye-holes might have filled with tears,
Had they been able. As it was,
With a glance at his all-seeing Boss,
He groaned, 'There'll be all Hell to pay – '
'Then *keep* it under your hat! Till the day
I'm ninety. Then I promise I'll come,'
And I crossed my heart to comfort him –
Which gave him such a shock I poured
Us both a big one. 'If I get bored,
I'll let you know,' I offered, to calm
His nerves, and took him by the arm,
But dropped it like an ice-cold curse.

He snickered: 'I'll send my Messengers.
Perhaps you'll change your mind.' With that,
He hop-skip-jumped and snatched his hat
From its holy hat-rack, where it hung
Battered and black, and drunkenly swung
Or lurched, with a curse, through my closed door.
When I unlatched it, Death was no more
To be seen. The night was black as pitch.
'Mind you don't fall in Hiasl's ditch!'
I hallooed after him. But he
Was gone where living eyes can't see."

– Presuming, dear sir, that Caspar, dressed
In his best *Lederhosen*, addressed
His *Kompagnons* at Gindlalm
In some such way; with scarcely a qualm,
Faced his own death full on; outstared
The Bone-man's grin; and even dared
To pit his wit against his power
By postponing for so long the hour
Of his arrival: with this tale,
Although still weak and 'unco pale',
His reputation as a sly fox
Was resurrected. When Death knocks
And enters, others leave feet first –
A fate which Caspar virtually reversed
By playing the Joker, as he came
To be known by many. Thus his fame,
Which, if not snuffed, had flickered and sunk
For the long dark months he'd spent as drunk
As Tam o'Shanter, spread as wide
As the city of Munich. When he died,
Some rhymes were found by his bed-side –
Among them this short palinode:

> *To My Bed*

Dear bed, in which I first began
To mewl and puke like any man,

To think and act – or act and think
And, later, drown my thoughts in drink;
Where, stiff with labour, I lie down
And rest my head on eider-down;
When sick, where my poor body lies
To soothe its pain with half-closed eyes;
Where, bowed by cares, I'll even weep
Before I sink into sweet sleep;
Where, long ago, I'd often find
The joys of man- and woman-kind
When Traudl still had all her charms,
Alive and warm in her husband's arms:
Life's centre, where its joy and pain,
Disease or ease, are routed or reign;
Since, in this little kingdom's space,
So many various scenes take place,
The lessons which it has to teach
Are more than books or priests can preach –
That nothing's perfect, good or ill
Are always mingled, do what you will,
While truth and lies which look the same
Depend on what's your aim or game…

Dear bed, where I shall cease to be
When once again Death comes for me.

The question, though, remained – of where
(If not, in fact, into thin air)
The old fox vanished. Though no church-goer,
He and Great-uncle Melchior
Were thick as thieves. The parish priest,
Downing a schnapps, would bless, at least,
The trout or game his brother had poached
Before they ate it. As Death approached
Again, old Caspar soaked up more
Than he had ever soaked before,
My father claimed, who (having downed
So much himself he might have drowned
In such a vasty vatful) tried,

Before he puked his liver and died,
To blame his thirst on the family tree,
One of whose branches, though, is me,
Who have no use for potent drink.
A poor performance, sir, I think,
To decline responsibility
And blame our weakness on those we
Should thank for our existence. Poor
Toni, declining more and more,
Blamed history: "Life's a rotten bitch,"
He'd mutter: "Look in Hiasl's ditch!
You'll find me next to my dead dad.
The Brandner family's gone from bad
To worse…" Or sometimes: "But the worst
Was covered up…" Convinced he was cursed,
He died at only seventy. We
Brandners lie in the cemetery
At Gmund, where Uncle Melchior
Was parish priest. Two years before
He'd buried Balthazar as well…
What really happened? Who can tell? –
But shortly before old Caspar died,
A girl was found, the promised bride
Of, yes, my father, trampled and crushed
By stampeding cows as they kicked and pushed
Across the ditch through a gap in the hedge
Under the pine-trees, at the edge
Of the forest, where they'd stand and shelter
From the raging, blinding, deafening welter
(To which they were accustomed, though)
Of Alpine thunderstorms. I know –
I've checked the records – this poor girl
Was so de-formed from heel to skull
("Severely disarticulated",
As the *post mortem* baldly stated)
That no one at first observed the cut
Into her lower belly. But
Neither could anyone explain
What, more than lightning, wind and rain,

Had panicked thirty cows so badly
They ignored her trusted voice and, madly,
Surged like a river in full flood
For half-a-mile through the storm-tossed wood,
Lowing and lost. When they grew calm,
The *Sennerin* of Gindlalm –
For she it was – lay dead in the mud,
Her tattered *Dirndl* thick with blood,
A victim of bad luck, what else?
The mournful clank of the same cow bells
Could still be heard as Balthazar
Behind his polished brass-topped bar
Parried the awkward chat of inquirers
Or curious hikers over the years.
I heard him more than once, when young,
Explaining how the girl was wrong –
Should have known better than to try
To stop them. What a way to die!
She should have kept well out of their way:
Much more than that he couldn't say…
Though once I overheard him add:

"The storm that day was very bad:
As Melchior, my brother, can verify,
While it was raging he and I,
Visiting Caspar, were forced to stay
Until it finally died away
Later that evening. I heard the news
At Gindlalm… With nothing to lose,
Some cat then spread the vicious lie
That the girl was pregnant – though who by
Nobody cared (or dared?) to imply:
A wicked rumour, who could doubt it?
Even her mother knew nothing about it.
Her fiancé Toni was away
Fighting the French. As sweet as May,
The *Sennerin* went to church, and read
Her Bible. After she was dead,
A girl-friend catted. Whereas in the story

Everyone's heard she goes to glory –
Now would St Peter have installed
An angel who'd been mucked and mauled
To sing God's praises? As for the wound
In her belly, which was only found –
Suspiciously, it seems to me –
Before her funeral, maybe we
Should treat the facts which the tale presents
As the truest version of events…" –

The tale which everyone prefers,
The one you've heard yourself, dear sir,
Which derived, however, from Melchior –
As I discovered shortly before
He died from my schnapps-sodden father;
Though, if you think, it's clear that neither
Caspar – its (missing) hero – nor
The Pearly Gates' saint / janitor,
The sanctified *Sennerin* nor Death,
Could then (if ever) have had the breath
To tell it… After Toni died,
I swallowed my agnostic pride
And took the steamer from Wiessee
To Gmund. What Melchior had to say,
Though aged (he confided) eighty-one,
Hid more than it revealed. He spun
His pious yarn in the shuttered gloom
Of his study. In that book-lined room,
With big old leather-bound dark tomes,
Biblical commentaries, prayer-books, poems,
Lit only by large candles, I
Felt overawed. In Melchior's eye
There might have been a twinkle, while
A knowing or malicious smile –
Except that he hardly had a tooth –
Insinuated, "*What is truth?*"
Until, before I realized,
I felt as good as hypnotized
By his white face and droning voice,

Appearing, weirdly, to have no choice
But to believe his flagrant fiction
And listen without contradiction
To fibs as if they were plain facts –
Though covering which nefarious tracks? –
Also to certain details, sir,
Of which you may not be aware.
I'll try to remember who he said
Did and said what. Now Melchior's dead
Himself at last – aged eighty-nine –
As the last of our tale-telling line,
With neither wife nor child, I intend
To bring it to an honest end…
Crossing himself, and also me,
He began by sacerdotally
Intoning, "My son, how good of you
To visit me. Yes, yes, it's true
St Peter sussed out Caspar… I
At sixty was too young to die
And returned with Death to tell the tale –
Which, after all, could hardly fail
To restore his image. From the start,
I omitted or played down my part,
For reasons of humility,
In Death and Caspar's comedy
And, now, don't get a mention. But
Since, it appears, you're plagued by doubt
And fear, my son, *re* final things,
Let me assure you, pigs have wings.
At least, my brother Caspar's soul
Flew further – higher – on the whole
Than almost anyone expected.
And proven truths must be respected –
The more so if attested by
The witness of a priestly eye…
The *Sennerin*, as you know, had died
Shortly before – the promised bride
Of Toni, marching far away
Or dead himself, perhaps. I'd say –

What with the death as well, in the war,
Of Georg, his firstborn, years before –
Caspar had just about had enough
Of illness, death, and such-like stuff.
The Bone-man's Messengers, he called them.
The *Sennerin's* end confused and appalled him.
I'd gone to try and calm him down,
When in through his closed door a clown
Shocked us by hopping. Almost at once
I recognized the 'Mr Bones'
Of Caspar's tale. 'But just a mo,'
Caspar complained: 'We agreed I'd go
At ninety. That's in ten years' time.'
Bones danced a little pantomime –
Glass – bottle – *pop!* – *glug*: 'Caspar, my friend,
I know when your stint is due to end –
Unless, that is, you've changed your mind…'
– 'Not yet… And yet…'
                        'I'm sure you'll find
Your last ten winters sheer delight.'
– 'You look like death. Are you all right?'
– 'I got the sack.'
                    'Oh hell – '
                                  'But then
St Peter took me on again –
After he'd wiped Heaven's floor with me –
Provided that… Well, let's say he
Agreed it would be worse than absurd
If Death were not to keep his word:
Why, then, should anybody else?'
– 'But how did he latch on?'
                              'A girl's
Sweet soul came knocking at Heaven's gate
And blew the gaff. Her gruesome fate
Fluttered his hard old porter's heart…
But perhaps it wasn't *very* smart,
Caspar, to tell the whole wide world
About our bet: the Porter hurled
His hard old keys at my numb skull,

90

Calling me *Bonehead! Drunken fool!*'
– Though neither he nor the girl had repeated,
Bones smarmed, the tale that Caspar *cheated*...
St Peter loved a *Dirndl*, and
A nice Bavarian brass-band:
She looked so *brav*, so innocent,
He enthused, that like a shot he sent
Her up to sing with wings in the Choir
Invisible, threatening Death with dire
Woe if he touched a drop again...
Whereon Bones grasped what seemed a pain
In his non-existent maw: 'But, perhaps,
Dear Caspar (you know what rhymes), a *schn-* - - -
Would really calm my nerves... And, don't worry,
No one's in any sort of hurry
About exactly when you die.
In fact, I was just passing by...
But won't you, now I'm here, at least – ?'
'Melchior – Bones, Bones – Melchior the priest,'
My brother, albeit somewhat gruffly,
Obliged. Death grinned and, bowing stiffly,
Hee-hawed, 'Oho, a man of G-d!'
And kissed my hand with a wink and a nod:
'Planning, perhaps, your life after death?' –
But had to pause to get his breath
After the *Obstler* Caspar had poured him.
A cough and splutter soon restored him
To the best of spirits: 'How can I
Repay such hospitality,
Caspar, my friend?... I'll tell you what:
You can't imagine the *Gaudi* you've got
Laid up forever in Paradise –'
'Well now, I've heard it's very nice –'
'It's heaven itself! Just like Bavaria,
But bluer and whiter, lighter and airier.
Your wife and elder son will be there
To greet you, and your Ma and Pa –'
'Why didn't you tell me this before?'
– 'You never asked. But at your door

My coach and horses wait for me:
We could go for a spin if you'd like to see
The treasure neither moth nor rust
Corrupts, when dust returns to dust –'
'Before I die?'
                'Why not? I know
A spec where you can wave hello –
A ha-ha of sorts – to the Blessed inside…'
I went along for the joy-ride –
Though, passing through a black storm-cloud,
Blinded by lightning, stunned by loud
And close-up claps of thunder, squished
Between my brother and Bones, I soon wished
I'd stayed at home. Before we arrived
At the ha-ha, which (Death joked) derived
From the gap in the wall which Satan smashed
When he and his rebel angels crashed
Out of the blue, we halted by
A peep-hole: 'Since the Blessed don't die,
And the Boss forgot to give me a soul,
I'm locked out, too. But this sweet hole
(I drilled it with my sting) lets me peep
At his beautiful angels.'
                     – '*Pfui*, you creep!
Drive on, drive on!' bold Caspar cried:
'Since most of my former family have died,
We'll have a fine *Familienfest!*' –
And on we drove. You know the rest:
St Peter let Caspar walk inside,
And when he met his wife he cried;
His parents and Georg also ran
To greet him. Heavenly bells began
To ring as sweetly as they rang
In Gmund. The blessed *Sennerin* sang
On high like yodelling down the wind.
And Caspar began to change his mind –
Till, when a cherub flew to say
Death was about to wing his way
Earthwards, he murmured he'd rather stay…

And that," concluded Melchior, "was that."
But if telling history tells us what
We'd like to happen, asking why
Tells us about ourselves... If we die,
Like Caspar, in a ditch, or worse,
The story which the world prefers
Will be a harmless *Märchen*. And yet
The truth is always present... But
Here come my pupils. Please forgive
Me if I finish now. To live
I work as a tutor. Which consumes
My life. But you, sir, I presume,
Will have more time...? Although my sort
Prefers to test what we've been taught –
Sift fact from fiction, *why* from *which* –
The truth needs time. And of those not rich,
Only the dead can neither want nor
Work. I remain
          Your servant,
               C. Brandner

Postscript

In the version of Brandner Caspar *which Franz von Kobell eventually published in 1871, the Tegernseer* Schlitzohr *and poacher swindles Death by getting him drunk, etc. – as in Caspar Brandner's letter. But no mention is made of the old man's drunkenness. Von Kobell also makes no mention of Balthazar or Melchior; the circumstances relating to the death of the* Sennerin *(who is merely attacked by an angry steer); the fact that the* Sennerin *was Toni's* Verlobte; *or the disappearance of Caspar's body. Both Georg and Toni have died fighting for the Fatherland, so that Toni's drunkenness and maudlin suspicions are omitted from the tale as well. Above all, there is no mention of the letter from Caspar Brandner (who died in 1870) which supplied von Kobell with much of his story. What remains, as Caspar Brandner unwittingly foresaw, is, precisely, a* "Schwank" *or* "harmless Märchen". *As well as suppressing or glossing over the question of* "What really happened? Who can tell?", *von Kobell turns Heaven into a pastoral idyll where Brandner Caspar is welcomed (with all his imperfections forgotten) by Toni, Georg, Traudl, his parents, friends, the angels and presumably God… In twentieth century versions of the tale, the after-life increasingly resembles Bavaria. The first for the stage was produced in Munich in 1934 and included the heroic death in battle of Caspar's sons. In another, light operatic version Death arrives not on a pale horse but, like the* Reichsmarschall *himself, in a little aeroplane. Shortly after the Second World War, the film* Der Brandner Caspar Schaut ins Paradies *(Brandner Caspar in Paradise) was a hit in the south of Germany. By this time the story's idea of Heaven was Bavaria itself… Only thirty years after the war had ended with the* Boanlkramer's *triumph over literally untold millions, the Munich* Nationaltheater, *looking for a Bavarian classic, decided on* Brandner Caspar, *and a new version was written for the stage in which Heaven is a village* Bierfest *with angels in* Lederhosen *partaking of beer,* Weißwurst *and* Bretzeln. *The Devil plays a role so minor that you miss him if you blink. Thirty years later still, with the war a distant memory, a revival at the Munich* Volkstheater *ran to (almost) universal acclaim. Only the oldest Bavarians now were alive at the time of the November Putsch or remember the rise of the Nazis and the SA in Munich and the surrounding countryside. Hitler himself was of course a great lover of the Bavarian mountains and picturesque lakes such as the Chiemsee and Brandner Caspar's Tegernsee. And so were other prominent members of the Party – for instance,* Reichsführer-SS *Himmler (a one-time chicken-farmer from Waldtrudering near Munich) and his boss, Ernst Röhm, the unruly and ambitious Chief of Staff of the SA. In fact, Röhm's ambitions came to an unruly end in the very village of Wiessee, on the Tegernsee, from which Caspar Brandner wrote his letter. Wiessee was in the meantime a spa town, and at the end of June 1934 Röhm and other SA leaders together with their hangers-on were taking a cure. In the years after Hitler himself had built it up in 1920–21, the SA had swollen to a private army of two-and-a-half million "brawling Brownshirts". Who knows whether Toni and Georg might not have joined it, had they been born in the twentieth century? As its long-standing leader, Röhm had become far too powerful and – even by Nazi standards – disreputable not only for Hitler but for the* Wehrmacht, *to say nothing of Göring and Himmler. The latter (the son of a school-teacher) was a fastidious and, if anything, even more ambitious man than Röhm himself was – a particularly ruthless in-fighter, whose SS was still no more than an arm of the SA.* Schlitzohr *as he also was, Hitler planned to get the* Wehrmacht *on the side of the Nazis by sacrificing Röhm, one of his closest friends in the movement – who had even done time with him in Stadelheim prison after the failure of the Beer Hall (November) Putsch in 1923*. He had accordingly presented Röhm with an ultimatum, to rein in and purge the SA or face the consequences, at the beginning of June. But Röhm declared, "The SA is and will remain the destiny of Germany." However, he invited Hitler to confer with the SA leadership on 30 June at Wiessee in the beautiful surroundings of the Führer's beloved Bavaria. When not ardently active in the cause, the hard-drinking Röhm – a First World War veteran, the upper part of whose nose had been shot away – enjoyed the company of young men, and Wiessee, with its spa and gambling casino, was a fine resort for a summer holiday. But Göring and Himmler, as his main political rivals, had been feeding Hitler with rumours of plotting and an imminent SA revolt, until the Führer *(whom no one has ever accused of cowardice)* kept his appointment in a way which Röhm can hardly be blamed for failing to foresee. William L. Shirer, who was in Germany at the time and, for all I know, watched the first stage production of Brandner Caspar *in Munich in the same year, describes events as follows:*

> At 2 a.m. on June 30th, as Hitler, with Goebbels at his side, was taking off from Hangelar Airfield near Bonn, Captain Röhm and his SA lieutenants were peacefully slumbering in their beds at the Hanslbauer Hotel at Wiessee on the shores of the Tegernsee. Edmund Heines, the SA Obergruppenführer *of Silesia, a convicted murderer, a notorious homosexual with a girlish face and the brawny body of a piano mover, was in bed with a young man. So far did the SA chiefs seem from staging a revolt that Röhm had left his staff guards in Munich. There appeared to be plenty of carousing among the SA leaders but no plotting.*
>
> Shortly after dawn Hitler and his party sped out of Munich towards Wiessee in a long column of cars. They found Röhm and his friends still fast asleep in the Hanslbauer Hotel. The awakening was rude. Heines and his young male companion were dragged out of bed, taken outside of the hotel and summarily shot on the orders of Hitler. The Führer *entered Röhm's room alone, gave him a dressing down and ordered him to be brought back to Munich and lodged in Stadelheim prison…*
>
> Hitler, in a final act of what he apparently thought was grace, gave orders that a pistol be left on the table of his old comrade. Röhm refused to make use of it. "If I am to be killed, let Adolf do it," he is reported to have said. Thereupon two SS officers entered the cell and fired their revolvers at Röhm point-blank.

At the same time in Berlin, Göring and Himmler had been busy removing their SA rivals, among others. In a Reichstag speech in July Hitler admitted to seventy-seven deaths in the purge, which he justified as necessary to stem revolt. However, in 1957, at the trial of Sepp Dietrich – who, "as one of the most brutal men in the Third Reich, commanded Hitler's SS Bodyguard in 1934 and directed the executions in Stadelheim prison" (Shirer) – the number of those who died was estimated at "more than 1,000"... If Der Brandner Caspar Schaut ins Paradies *had catered to the Bavarian idea of Heaven as Bavaria, trials such as Dietrich's showed clearly enough that the same idyllic countryside had once been – and, like any other idyllic countryside, could become again – a department of Hell.*

v

Case Studies, 1941–1945

"The most primitive man says that the horse is good and the bedbug bad, or wheat is good and the thistle bad. The human being, consequently, designates what is useful to him as good and what is harmful as bad..."
Himmler, Minsk, 31 Aug. 1942

(i)

SS-Standartenführer Rudolf Brandt,
Persönlicher Referent des Reichsführers-SS

Today he wanted a batch of a hundred shot –
to observe a 'liquidation' – so as to know
what it was like. One blond-haired boy stood out,
with eyes (he told me) of piercing Aryan blue.

He stopped them: "Jewish?" – "Yes" – "Both parents?" – "Yes" –
"Non-Jewish forbears?" – "No" – "Then I can't help..." –
stepped back, and dropped his eyes... Two young Jewesses
were still alive. He yelled out, "*Shoot!* don't torment them!"

Afterwards he made a speech. This repulsive duty
must be fulfilled – though never, by Germans, with pleasure.

He hated blood. But the full responsibility,
after deep thought, was his – before God and Hitler.

He encouraged the *Einsatzgruppe* to think of Nature:
a world of combat. At the top, the Germans.
The weak go under – bedbugs, lice. The strongest nurture
what keeps them strong – exterminate vermin.

*

Rudolf Brandt, 1909–1948, was Himmler's 'Personal Administrative Officer' from 1937 until the Reichsführer's *death in May 1945. A lawyer by profession, Brandt was described by another of Himmler's closest associates, his head of foreign intelligence, Walter Schellenberg, as "the eyes and ears of his master". Schellenberg observed the ways in which Brandt made himself useful: "Because of his ability as a perfect stenographer, his punctuality, his untiring diligence, he became Himmler's omnipresent and indispensable registering, reminding and writing machine, complaining about being overworked and yet declaring with pride that he had to produce 3,000–4,000 out-going letters per month." Among these letters were a number concerning Himmler's "many lunacies" (Shirer) with regard to medical and other experiments, the organization and coordination of some of which Brandt attended to on behalf of his busy chief. After the war, he was charged in the so-called 'Doctors' Trial' at Nuremberg with "performing medical experiments without the subjects' consent on prisoners of war and civilians of occupied countries". Although he had not, of course, performed experiments in person, a note appended to his affidavit concerning his positions in the Nazi party and the SS includes the comment, "By virtue of his position as administrative assistant to Himmler, Rudolf Brandt played a very significant role in practically all of the crimes with which this case is concerned." He was found guilty, and hanged on 2 June 1948.*

(ii)

SS-Obergruppenführer Erich von dem Bach

I did my duty. But, when Himmler ordered
the squad to carry out orders unconditionally,

and keep their conscience clear, his 'good' and 'bad'
were whose? His? Ours? His horrified cry

amazed them. *Herr Reichsführer, that was a hundred,*
I told him: *Look in their eyes. What sort of future
are we creating? Look. These men are done for
as men. Soon they'll be mad, or savage...*

But the shootings broke *me* down. I re-lived our 'work'
in lurid time-loops. As *'eisener Heinrich'*, he liked
my ruthless side, and brought his top doctor: *Get back
for both our sakes. And the Führer's...* But we lied

about the Jews. Our propaganda claimed
this race of helpless, hopeless losers was
helping the Russians, whom they feared. Word came:
Try quicker, cleaner methods. Dynamite. Gas.

*

***Erich von dem Bach**, 1899–1972, was Higher SS and Police Leader, Central Russia. From June 1941 he was in charge of numerous killing operations in Eastern Europe – a task which, according to Raul Hilberg in* The Destruction of the European Jews, *led to a breakdown which seems to have been as much mental as physical (he was operated on for serious stomach and intestinal complaints). Back in action in Eastern Europe, where he was engaged in the hopeless fight against Polish and Russian partisans, he disagreed with Himmler over the latter's recommendation that entire villages should be burned down if need be, insisting that "no country can be ruled by police and troops alone" and arguing for a less brutal and less alienating policy which would make use of the Poles' dislike of communism and encourage them to side with the Germans. Nevertheless, Hitler, who regarded him as "one of the cleverest people", and whom he never questioned as his* Führer, *demanded "the most brutal means possible" during the anti-partisan sweeps of 1942 and '43 – and in Belorussia, where von dem Bach was in command, the death-rate soared. When his men were unable to trap the partisans themselves, hundreds of civilians – many of them Jews – would be shot at a time, leaving heaps of corpses in burning villages. Belorussia later struck an American journalist as "the most devastated* *country in Europe" (Mark Mazower,* Hitler's Empire*). More than one in four members of the population died (about 345,000 civilians and 30,000 partisans) and 9,000 villages were burned to the ground. However, von dem Bach's ability to do his repulsive duty appears not always to have blinded him to how things were, and he testified with unusual and disarming honesty at Nuremberg regarding "the greatest lie of anti-Semitism", namely "that the Jews are conspiring to dominate the world and that they are so highly organized. In reality, they had no organization of their own at all, not even an information service. If they had had some sort of information, these people could have been saved by the million; but instead they were taken completely by surprise. Never before has a people gone so unsuspectingly to its disaster. Nothing was prepared. Absolutely nothing."*

(iii)

SS-Obergruppenführer Reinhard Heydrich

Am Großen Wannsee, Berlin, 20 Jan. 1942

Mental Notes for Conference re *Jewish Question*

1   *Solutions so far*

1.1   Definition of Jewishness – 'Law for the Protection of German Blood and Honour', 1935 (too lenient, too detailed, letting too many *Mischlinge* off the hook)

1.2 Ghettoization: to concentrate Jewish population – sever contacts between Jews and Germans – restrict their housing – control their movement – enforce identification measures – set up and regulate Jewish administrative machinery, culminating in *Reichsvereinigung der Juden in Deutschland* (Feb. 1939)

– Gestapo empowered to issue orders to *Reichsvereinigung* (July 1939) and all other Jewish councils: senior Jews held personally responsible for communal compliance

– Almost all Jews in Eastern Europe now in actual ghettos or equivalent: Warsaw, Lódz, Kraków, Lublin, Lwów, Theresienstadt, etc. etc.

2   *"Endlösung der Judenfrage"*

2.1 Estimated number of Jews (incl. England and Ireland) to be liquidated: 11 million

2.2 Authorization for SS to proceed with 'Final Solution' across all European and former Soviet territories: drafted by Eichmann, signed by Göring, 31 July 1941 [all conference participants to bow to this *coup]*

2.3 *Methods to be employed*

2.3.1 'SS to victims': *Einsatzgruppen* – mobile execution squads in former Soviet territory – Jews to be liquidated on the spot – launched June 1941, in conformity with 'guide-lines' from the *Führer*

2.3.2 'Victims to SS': deportations to Eastern Europe in operation since Oct. 1941 – Jews as forced labour (building roads, repairing railways) – many eliminated by natural causes – survivors to be subjected to 'special treatment'

2.3.3 Concentration camps equipped with carbon monoxide gassing installations – tested late 1941 at Chelmno (Kulmno), using gas-vans

2.3.4 Building of Brackian devices (gas-chambers) in process or planned at Belzec, Sobibór, Treblinka, using carbon monoxide (mainly) – bodies to be buried in mass graves

2.3.5 Quicker, more efficient gas than carbon monoxide (experiments at Auschwitz, Sept. 1941)? Easier, more efficient disposal of bodies than mass burial or burning in the open?

*

Reinhard Heydrich, 1904–1942, was Himmler's deputy. Among many other crimes, Heydrich had been the main organizer, at Goebbels' instigation and with Hitler's permission, of the infamous pre-war pogrom known as Reichskristallnacht, *9–10 Nov. 1938, in which at least 400 German and Austrian Jews died at once and many more later. In all, about 30,000 were transported to concentration camps, 1,500 synagogues were gutted, and 7,500 Jewish properties vandalized or destroyed. As for the Wannsee conference, Heydrich insisted that it be kept top secret, and there was very possibly no written agenda. The only record of what was said is a single surviving copy of Eichmann's minutes, which are certainly incomplete (Eichmann testified at his trial in Jerusalem in 1961 that he had been ordered to "clean up" in particular the last twenty minutes of the conference – which he summarized in one bland and evil sentence: "In conclusion, the different types of possible solutions were discussed")... As ruthless a careerist as his boss, with exceptional clarity of administrative vision, Heydrich was assassinated near Prague only a few months after the meeting at Wannsee – for which an estimated 4,500 people were killed in reprisals. But he had done his diabolical worst. In the face of opposition from the Interior Ministry, the Foreign Ministry, the Eastern Ministry and the representative of Hans Frank's General Government, Heydrich got what he wanted at Wannsee, namely the agreement of all participants that Himmler, Heydrich and the SS were to be "entrusted with the official central handling of the final solution of the Jewish question without regard to borders". Heydrich achieved this by sheer force of personality plus fast thinking but also by means of Göring's letter of authorization, which was news to most of those present and which he read out in full. The authorization concluded with the ominous words, "I charge you furthermore with submitting to me in the near future an overall plan of the organizational, functional, and material measures to be taken in preparing for the implementation of the aspired final solution of the Jewish question"... Although he rarely drank, Heydrich is said to have permitted himself a small cognac in celebration of this – the biggest SS power-grab since the death of Röhm.*

(iv)

Heinz Auerswald, Kommisar für den
Jüdischen Wohnbezirk, Warschau

The Jews lacked work, lacked food, lacked warmth, lacked strength
to help themselves. One doctor wrote to me –
not long before nine tenths of the ghetto were sent
to be 'resettled' – that energetic, busy

persons reverted to listless, sleepy
half-wits, too *schlapp* to get up to piss
or clean themselves, and drifting (though less slowly
than in old age) towards death, with breath-rate and pulse

subsiding – nothing violent, no real pain.
Those who found food could scarcely chew or digest it.
Heart, liver, kidneys, spleen all shrink. The skin
withers, awareness fades. Death in the street

was common. He needed money. We didn't have it,
and wouldn't have sent it if we had. Our view
was let the *Judenrat* put up its taxes:
Jews always relish blaming other Jews.

*

Heinz Auerswald, 1908–1970, was an SS lawyer and police officer until his career in Berlin and Poland peaked in 1940–41 when he was transferred to the civilian administration of Warsaw and promoted to Commissar of the Warsaw Ghetto. He occupied this post until transferred again, into the Wehrmacht, *in Jan. 1943, presumably because Himmler had decided on the total dissolution of what was left of the ghetto – thus provoking, quite unexpectedly, the famous Jewish armed resistance of April–May. Apart from this last battle, Auerswald presided over the establishment, day-to-day administration and systematic evacuation of this largest of Nazi ghettos. He is said to have been polite but heartless and to have insisted that 'punishment actions' against Jews be carried out by the Jewish Council, whose chairman,*

Adam Czerniaków, eventually killed himself. Jewish ghetto councils were also forced by the German authorities to raise funds from taxes – for example, on those who worked, those who were exempt from work, postal services, rents, rationed bread, medicines, and even cemeteries. As recorded in Claude Lanzmann's Shoah, *the cemetery tax was one reason why there were so many corpses on the streets: their families could not afford to bury them. Typically, the Jewish councils were blamed instead of the Nazis, as Reinhardt Heydrich clearly intended when setting up the administrative machinery of the Final Solution: "When deficiencies occur," Auerswald noted with evident satisfaction, "the Jews direct their resentment against the Jewish administration, and not against the German supervision."*

Meanwhile, the ghettos were being emptied by deportation – again through the agency of the Jewish councils. In Warsaw, the main deportations took place in 1942. In the end, most of the ghetto's original 445,000 inhabitants perished, either through 'Aussiedlung' (resettlement) in Treblinka and elsewhere or in the ghetto itself. In fact, conditions in the Polish ghettos were allowed to deteriorate to so atrocious a level, and the ratio of births to deaths was so low, that no more than 5% of their original populations would still have been alive twenty-five years later. But, of course, this was hardly fast enough for the Germans. Hence the death-camps.

(v)

Hermann Friedrich Gräbe, Dipl. Ing.

We needed workers – to fulfil our contracts.
The Jews were skilled. I saved perhaps a hundred.
At Dubno, though, the SS killed 5,000 –
behind our building site. Our foreman showed me

the mounds of earth – trucks – naked Jews – their clothing
and shoes in heaps – Ukrainian militia – Germans
with whips and clubs. Suddenly, machine-gun clatter.
Large families tried to comfort one another

and say goodbye – one father speaking softly
to a boy of ten – a white-haired grandmother singing

to a laughing baby. A slender girl moved past me,
pointed to herself and murmured, "Twenty-three."

Behind the mound an SS man sat smoking,
the gun across his knees. A thousand bodies
lay massed in a ditch. Some moved. Those next consoled them.
Three locals, watching, waited. One raised his camera.

*

Hermann Friedrich Gräbe, 1900–1986, was manager and chief engineer of the Sdolbunow branch (Ukraine) of the Josef Jung Construction Company, Solingen, from Sept. 1941 to June 1944. The company was building, among other things, grain warehouses for the Wehrmacht *at the Dubno airfield. The unadorned directness, courage and compassion of Gräbe's sworn affidavit at Nuremberg made him enemies in post-war Germany, where – as W.L. Shirer noted in a related context – "most Germans, at least as far as their sentiment was represented in the West German parliament, did not approve of even the relatively mild sentences meted out to Hitler's accomplices. A number of those handed over by the Allies to German custody were never prosecuted, even when accused of mass murder, and some of them found employment in the Bonn government." As late as the 1990s, W.G. Sebald (who left Germany for England in 1966) wrote with distaste in* The Emigrants *of "the mental impoverishment and lack of memory that marked the Germans, and the efficiency with which they had cleaned everything up". In this society, which was clearly in a state of growing denial, Gräbe suffered harassment of various kinds. Unable to find work, he left Germany with his family for California, where he later died. His efforts at saving Jews included falsifying documents, inventing projects for which he needed workers, and warning them of SS operations. He was honoured by the state of Israel as 'Righteous among the Nations'. As for the 5,000 killed at Dubno, these will have been among the 90,000 Jews whom Otto Ohlendorf, commander of* Einsatzgruppe D, *which was active in the Ukraine, admitted at Nuremberg that his group had summarily executed. Generally speaking, Ohlendorf had preferred firing squads to shooting by individuals, because the latter "both for the victims and for those who carried out the shooting was, psychologically, an immense burden to bear".*

(vi)

SS-Sturmbahnführer Konrad Morgen, Dr. jur.

Knowing the rampant power of rumours, the Gestapo
moved to eradicate this one. But too late.
The New York Times reported how the Germans
were using the fat of Jews for making soap.

This sapped morale. Worse still, it threatened to leak
our secret *Lösung*. Ordered at once by Müller
to sniff out more, my attention was soon directed
to *Sonderkommando Dirlewanger's* (alleged)

excessive cruelty. It seems young Jewish women
were rounded up and stripped. Injected with strychnine,
they writhed and choked, while 'Gandhi' and cronies watched.
The bodies, cut in pieces, were then boiled

together with horse-meat into grease or soap…
They plundered – gang-raped – tortured – whipped to death…,
but the case was never tried. The *Kommando* was posted
to Russia. Too tough a task-force. Too keen on terror.

*

Konrad Morgen*, 1909–1982, was a judge and SS investigator. Morgen testified at Nuremberg that, with direct authority from Himmler, he investigated about 800 cases of SS corruption and other abuses: "About 200 were tried as a result of my activities. Five concentration camp commandants were arrested by me personally. Two were shot after being tried… Apart from the commandants, there were numerous other death sentences against SS-Führers and -Unterführers." He claimed that Hitler's euthanasia policy and the Final Solution were beyond his jurisdiction. After the war he continued his legal career in Frankfurt. As for the soap rumour,* The New York Times *reported it on 26 Nov. 1942, quoting as its source a statement by Rabbi Dr Stephen Wise, Chairman of the World Jewish Congress. In fact the rumour, like other reports which reached the* *outside world with regard to the extermination of the Jews, was treated with suspicion – at least to begin with. After the war, however, the story was widely believed and, according to J. Neander* (Seife und Judenfett, *2004), is still current in one form or another. Clearly, legends of this sort reflect some sort of reality. At Nuremberg the Russians even produced a 'recipe' which they alleged had been used in Danzig. By sending Konrad Morgen to investigate, Himmler and Heinrich Müller, chief of the Gestapo, conceded that there was at least the possibility of 'experiments' by the likes of Oskar Dirlewanger (1895–1945), whose* Sonderkommando *had been created by Himmler personally – on the Romantic medieval model of Heinrich I, who employed a company of convicted poachers. It has been estimated that Dirlewanger spent seventeen years of his working life in active service (after the First World War, he fought in the Spanish Civil War and for paramilitary groups). Otherwise, he worked in business, which he had studied, and as a tax advisor. A convicted rapist and child-abuser, he was a notorious sadomasochist but also an effective task-force leader, answerable to Himmler directly. His men were mainly ex-convicts, released from gaol on condition that they fight. Himmler gave Dirlewanger extra-judicial power of life and death over his troops, a right which he used sparingly. He seems to have been highly respected by his regiment of criminal outsiders, who eventually numbered 6,500. His emaciated appearance earned him the nickname 'Gandhi'. From 1943,* Sonderkommando *Dirlewanger was engaged in Erich von dem Bach's anti-partisan campaign in Russia. No doubt they will have appealed to the latter's "ruthless side" (see (ii)).*

(vii)

Curzio Malaparte, War Correspondent,
Corriere della Sera

I looked away. And looked. This had to be
set down: the high street, Jassy, the morning after
the pogrom, from my window – bodies piled
in gutters – lying, sitting, kneeling – twisted

grotesquely – several hundred roughly dumped
in the churchyard. A child – dead head on shoulder – leaning

against a shop-front. Jews unblocking the road
for trucks, full of their dead. And laughing gypsies

running to get their share. Some pulled off shoes,
feet jammed against dead bellies; some stripped corpses,
made off with arms piled high. A merry bustle –
a colourful Romanian fair – a German market.

Whereas, as if afraid to step on hands
or bloody faces, packs of dogs went sniffing
the bodies with tender care – in search of lost
or dying masters, moved by pity.

*

Curzio Malaparte, 1898–1957, was a prolific Italian author and journalist. Malaparte was by turns a free-thinking fascist, republican, communist, Catholic, and not infrequently in trouble with the authorities. Nevertheless, he worked as a special correspondent for Corriere della Sera *during the war, following and reporting in daily articles on 'Operation Barbarossa' in 1941–42 and angering both the Fascists and the Nazis by saying what he saw. The novel* Kaputt *(1944), based on his experiences, is in fact a 'Self-Portrait as an Italian Officer' and amply exemplifies this genre's capacity for criticizing not only the role in question but oneself for playing it: the narrator, 'Malaparte', is a self-disgusted participant in as well as (relatively) detached observer of the decadence of fascist Europe – he does not, however, participate in its brutality. The writing is uneven in quality, but there are many unforgettable and intensely imagined scenes, including an account of the opening gambit in the* Conductor *General Antonescu's 'master-plan' to rid Romania of its Jews, the massacre at Jassy (or Iasi) in 1941. Although a work of fiction,* Kaputt *incorporates incidents which have been accepted as historically accurate. Malaparte commented in his preface to the book, "Nothing can convey better than this hard, mysterious German word,* Kaputt *– which literally means 'broken, finished, gone to pieces, gone to ruin' – the sense of what we are, what Europe is: a pile of rubble."*

(viii)

SS-Obersturmbahnführer Eduard Strauch

Rough draft of letter to von dem Bach re *Generalkommissar Kube:*

And he praised my work at first: 55,000
'partisan helpers' (Jews) shot in ten weeks –
"The bestial hordes" he called them, proudly showing
his guests the church in Minsk stuffed full with their luggage...

We then shot seventy who had worked in his offices,
removing their gold teeth first in the proper way...
He called us sadists, ignorant young barbarians –
some had been German Jews, or Great War veterans,

lovers of Mendelssohn and Offenbach,
from the same cultural circles as himself...
I said they were just a few Jews. He objected violently
to our driving women, "covered with blood" (!), through the streets,

and other acts beneath a German man
and the Germany of Kant and Goethe... Kube
has clearly favoured and protected Jewry...
I beg to recommend his prompt dismissal.

*

***Eduard Strauch**, 1906–1955, was senior officer of* Einsatzkommando 2 *within* Einsatzgruppe A – *whose commander, however, was dissatisfied with Strauch's unreliable and impulsive behaviour, frequently under the influence of alcohol. Erich von dem Bach described him as the nastiest person he had come across in his life* ("dem übelsten Menschen dem ich in meinem Leben begegnet bin"). *In Nov. 1941, Strauch and twenty of his men murdered 10,600 Jews in Riga. His superior in Minsk,* Generalkommissar Wilhelm Kube, *described himself as a "hard man" and willing to deal with the Jewish problem. However, Strauch's behaviour seems to have precipitated a crisis of conscience in Kube, which grew sufficiently embarrassing in so high-*

ranking an official as to earn him a "serious warning" from the Ministry of the Occupied Eastern Territories in Berlin. To Himmler's relief, Kube was blown up by a bomb placed under his bed by a maidservant working for the Belorussian resistance, since as far as the Reichsführer *was concerned his Jewish policy had "bordered on treason". Nevertheless, Belorussia had been so devastated under Kube and von dem Bach that even post-war relief workers who had seen Germany and Poland were shocked by the scale of the destruction.*

(ix)

Walter Stier, Generaldirektion der Ostbahn, Sonderzüge

*After the war, in Frankfurt, his career
really took off, until at last he became
the* Bundesbahn's *new Head of Operations.
During the war, he'd never left his desk,*

*firstly in Kraków – "Close to Auschwitz? yes, I think
it was" – and then in Warsaw, where the Jews
had fought for once, though Lódz and other ghettos
were still to go. Not that he or his colleagues*

*knew or wanted to know what sort of passengers
filled the 'resettlement trains' for Belzec, Treblinka…
He worked on complex schedules. Some long trains –
say, fifty cattle-trucks – took hours to empty…*

*The fares were fixed per track-kilometer.
Groups of 400 travelled half-price – small children
for free – most tickets single. The SS
footed the bill – he thinks with the Jews' own money.*

*

Walter Stier, *1906–1985, was Head of 'Special Passenger Trains', Gedob –
"an important railway system with major functions in the destruction of the*

Jews" (Hilberg) – from Jan. 1940 in Kraków, then from 1943 in Warsaw. His department was responsible for the schedules of trains transporting Jews to the death-camps of Poland. He discusses his work and post-war career with Claude Lanzmann in Shoah, insisting that he had never actually seen a so-called 'rez`settlement train', and that no one in his right mind asked unnecessary questions. He concedes that there were rumours. Eichmann pointed out, at his trial in Jerusalem, that the construction of such schedules was a science in itself, and Stier is clearly proud of his expertise. Exactly how murderous this could be in practice is recorded, for example, in Night *by Elie Wiesel: of the hundred or so 'passengers' ("we were so skinny!") crammed into Wiesel's wagon from Auschwitz to Buchenwald, only twelve survived the journey. The railway system as a whole, without which the Final Solution would not have been possible, has been analysed by Hilberg.* Lanzmann, in his note on Walter Stier, confirms one of Hilberg's principal conclusions: "What happened could not have happened without a general consensus of the German people. This business was not the doing of a few gangsters. It called for the commitment of the entire bureaucratic and managerial apparatus of a great modern state."

(x)

SS-Oberscharführer Kurt Franz, Kommandant von Treblinka

I wrote this for the Jews to keep them happy:

"All in step we stride with our eyes straight ahead,
Always brave and free, with a spring in our tread
    To our work! We *Kommandos* are marching.

   For us there is only Treblinka,
   Where we are destined to be.
   That's why we felt at home in Treblinka
   So quickly and easily.

We wait on every word of our Commander,
With duty and obedience every day!

We want to serve and go on serving
Until the hour our luck runs out, hurray!"

And if the dogs forgot to howl it, Barry taught them.

*

Kurt Franz, 1914–1998, was Commandant of Treblinka. Franz was one of the most sadistic and feared of concentration camp commandants. After the war, he escaped from American custody and registered himself as unemployed in his own name (a common one) in his home-town of Düsseldorf, where he then worked as a cook – his original profession – until he was finally arrested in 1959. He was tried in the 'Treblinka Case' and sentenced to life-imprisonment for multiple murder and attempted murder. The court commented on his "well-nigh satanic cruelty", his "extraordinary criminal energy" and "mercilessness towards his victims". Among many other acts of "useless violence" (Primo Levi, The Drowned and the Saved), *it emerged that Franz would set his dog, Barry, on any prisoner he took a dislike to. Since Barry was the size of a calf, this resulted in most cases in the prisoner being no longer able to work and Franz or a medical orderly would shoot him… The song translated here is sung (twice) by the former SS-Unterscharführer, Franz Suchomel, in Lanzmann's* Shoah. *The words, according to Suchomel (who was a guard at Treblinka from Aug. 1942 to Oct. 1943), were written by Franz himself, while "the melody came from Buchenwald", where Franz had been a guard. All working Jews were to learn and be able to sing the song. Suchomel's comment on his rendition of it is: "That's unique. No Jew alive today can sing it"* (Das ist ein Original. Das kann keine Jude heute mehr). *Between 12,000 and 15,000 people a day were killed at Treblinka – altogether over a million – including most of those transported from the Warsaw ghetto.*

(xi)

**Diplom Kaufmann Hans Biebow,
Amtsleiter Ghettoverwaltung, Lódz**

I took pride in my work. Our virtual expropriation

of thieving Jewry; the exemplary productivity,
under the circumstances, of eighty-six factories;
the rationalization of their surplus labour

to only the fit – no kids, or sick, or old folk –
my motto *More with less*, theirs *Work will save us*.
My finest hour, though, was my speech to the strikers
in Workshops I and II: "Workers of the ghetto,"

I began, "you know I have always done my utmost
to keep you safe here. But Russian bombs are falling,
and this one last trans-shipment of you all
is simply meant to help you. German workers

have left for the front: Krupp, Daimler-Benz, and Siemens
need you. If you fight, there'll be dead and wounded.
So, common sense. Bring forty pounds of luggage –
food's on the trains. Now Lódz, tomorrow Deutschland!"

*

Hans Biebow, 1902–1947, was Head of Ghetto Administration, Lódz. A successful grain- and coffee-merchant, Biebow got on well with Reinhard Heydrich, through whom he became head of what was the second-largest ghetto in Poland. Lódz was a highly industrialized city – once known as 'the Polish Manchester'. Under Biebow's business-like leadership the factories of the ghetto made a sizeable profit, although its living conditions – largely because of his extreme unwillingness to spend money on food, hygiene or medicine – were among the worst in Poland. Two Czech survivors later remembered: "Excrement flowed along the pavements. When we arrived we found courtyards filled with refuse and in a state of total neglect. Only when epidemics threatened, did the Germans remove any rubbish... Cholera, jaundice and typhus were a constant danger. Everywhere people were dying of hunger and disease. We were four people to a room, with two plank beds and thousands of bugs, which it was impossible to get rid of. Bugs, fleas, lice. In the long queues to get food, the lice sprang from one person to another, carrying typhus fever. For the starving and exhausted people, it was terribly difficult (schrecklich schwer) *in winter to keep oneself clean. When we arrived we were offered some sort of turnip soup, which we were unable to eat, but others begged us for it. Later we ate it too. The hunger was the worst: young and old died of hunger."*

The slogan "Work will save us" (Unserer einzige Weg ist Arbeit) *appears to have been the invention of the president of the Jewish* Ältestenrat, *Chaim Rumkowski, who was directly answerable to Biebow. No doubt Heydrich had explained the principle of* Judenrat *responsibility (see (iii) and (iv)) to Biebow when he appointed him. Rumkowski has been much blamed and derided for behaving like a little* Führer. *However, the productivity of the Lódz ghetto was such that he can perhaps be excused for imagining that working hard might save at least some of his people. Raul Hilberg has convincingly described what was probably a general, though futile, policy of* Judenräte *everywhere – to sacrifice some so as to save some. In the first five months of 1942 about 55,000 of the 205,000 inhabitants of the ghetto were 'resettled'. Most of them died in or on the way to Chelmno (see (xii)). From 1–12 Sept. Biebow concentrated on making the ghetto more cost effective by closing the hospitals and transporting most of its old people and children under the age of ten. However, work saved nobody and in May 1944 Himmler gave the order for the ghetto's final dissolution. A sort of sit-down strike ensued, and Biebow made his speech on 7 Aug. The strikers were deceived, capitulated, and were transported to Chelmno, only fifty miles away, or to Auschwitz-Birkenau. In the end, no more than 5–6,000 of the ghetto's inhabitants escaped death.*

(xii)

Simon Srebnik, Sonderkommando, Chelmno

In their garden in Tel Aviv, surrounded by children,
his wife asks why look back. But he decides
to return to where, in the wood, they fed the ovens
with corpses from the gas-vans. Each full load,

after a night half-starved in Chelmno church,
was gassed in transit. Some, he remembers, were burned
while still alive: "Schnell! Schnell!" – with no time to search
among the tangled bodies. No one returned

in the swilled van. He laboured there six months,
inured to death from the ghetto. A boy, he survived
by singing for SS men – could run and hunt
like a dog. Though his parents died, he knew he'd live –

and, shot, the bullet passed straight through. He hid
in a pig-sty. Two dreams helped: one of five loaves.
Then of being left alone in the world. The loud crowd
of church-going Poles can't touch him. Alone. Alive.

*

Simon Srebnik, *1930–2006, was a member of the Jewish forced-labour squad in the 'forest camp' at Chelmno. As one of two known survivors of the camp, Srebnik was a witness at Eichmann's trial in 1961. In 1978, Claude Lanzmann persuaded him to go back to Chelmno, where he was remembered by the Polish villagers as "the singing boy". The opening of the poem describes a scene which was edited out of* Shoah.

Chelmno was the first German killing centre in Poland, six weeks or so before the Wannsee conference (see (iii)). The first phase was from 8 Dec. 1941 until March 1943. The Jews came mostly from nearby towns and villages and then from the Lódz ghetto. The forest camp was re-opened in June 1944 to facilitate what Biebow called the final 'Verlagerung' (trans-shipment) of the ghetto. This was when Simon Srebnik arrived, as a thirteen-year-old boy, having seen his father shot by the SS in Lódz. His mother was gassed in one of the vans. The gas-vans remained in use until the camp was closed in Jan. 1945. At least 150,000 people died there. Although Lanzmann insists that Shoah *is about death, not survival, Simon Srebnik – who was shot through the neck by the SS and found half-dead by the Russians two days later – is among the film's most extraordinary 'resurrections'.*

(xiii)

Jerzy Kubicki, KZ-Außenkommando Mannheim-Sandhofen

At first we were afraid the whole of Warsaw –

its Poles, like its Jews – would be reduced to ashes.
But, after the fighting, some were spared – for work
in the Reich. At Dachau, men in dark suits

drove up and chose us. Ah, but Daimler-Benz
was worse than Buchenwald, one ex-con said:
worse hours, more beatings, colder. Such meagre rations
that three months later hundreds were sick or dead.

The front drew near, but still we starved – slaved – froze.
Poor or slow work meant 'sabotage', which meant death.
The sirens wailed – bombs fell – and our hopes rose.
But Marian Krainski's show-trial cut them off.

This harmless, worried barber, and father of four –
ill-trained – made some slight error at his machine,
for which the management and SS hanged him
in the playground of the school where some of us slept.

*

Jerzy Kubicki, 1925–1986, was a member of the Polish external forced-labour squad at Mannheim-Sandhofen concentration camp. Kubicki is unusual in having written a memoir for his family about his experiences in Germany, as recorded by P. Koppenhöfer (in Das Daimler-Benz Buch, *1987). Of course, Daimler-Benz was not the only firm to use forced labour. Others were Heinkel, BMW, Krupp, Volkswagen, Siemens and Porsche. In* The Drowned and the Saved, *Primo Levi mentions that IG Farben actually owned Auschwitz-Monowitz. By the end of 1944, an estimated 420,000 prisoners were working for the German war economy, and the SS and German industry were co-operating in their exploitation. Jerzy Kubicki and his fellow-prisoners came from around Warsaw. Himmler welcomed the ill-timed Warsaw Uprising of July-Sept. 1944 as offering an opportunity to destroy the city permanently, as Hitler wished. Erich von dem Bach took command of all troops fighting the Poles from Aug. 1944 in a campaign which led to the deaths of 15,000 Home Army fighters together with 185,000 Polish civilians. Unlike the Jews of the ghettos, many surviving prisoners were young and fit, and around 150,000 were in fact transported to labour camps inside Germany, leaving Warsaw ruined and as good as deserted (the Germans continued to blow up public buildings, palaces, museums and libraries until only hours before the Russians arrived in Jan. 1945)... By about Dec. 1944, Daimler-Benz had no further use for its concentration camp workers and many were transported elsewhere, some of them to die at the so-called* 'Krankenlager Vaihingen'. *Sick prisoners were expensive and unproductive, and Mannheim was keen to be rid of them, "so that they should not be a burden on us unnecessarily"* (damit sie uns nicht unnötig belasten), *as one managerial directive expressed it. By Jan. 1945, only about 300 of the original 1,060 prisoners were still at Sandhofen, all in a precarious state of health. As elsewhere, the brutality and "useless violence" of the SS – in Mannheim with the assistance of Daimler-Benz – continued until the very end. The case of the Polish worker Marian Krainski later came before the American authorities. Krainski was accused by his departmental head, Karl Platzer, of 'sabotage' in Nov. 1944. All the signs point to Krainski's having dropped his template, which shifted by several hundredths of a millimetre without his noticing, so that the axles his machine was producing came out too thin. The SS demanded that the Deputy Works Manager, Robert Staffin (see (xiv)) report the matter in writing to Berlin, which he must (or should) have known could lead to Krainski's execution. The show-trial was conducted in front of the assembled KZ prisoners on 3 Jan. 1945, and Krainski was hanged the next day in the presence of Staffin, Platzer and other representatives of the firm.*

(xiv)

Direktor Robert Staffin, Stellvertretender Betriebsleiter, Daimler-Benz Mannheim

I blame top management. The *Wehrmacht* needed
6,000 Opel-Blitz *Dreitonner*, and quickly.
Opel was bombed in August. Daimler-Benz,
licensed to co-produce them, was short of workers.

Personell swung some deal with the Gestapo,
and a thousand fairly fit, young 'Warsaw bandits'
were picked up cheap in Dachau. But too many
were poorly trained. What's more, the war was lost:

no one expected that we'd need these workers
after, say, February 1945.
And so no money was spent to feed – clothe – house them.
Exhausted by twelve-hour shifts, they drooped and shuffled,

until some factory *Führer* shouted 'Sabotage!'
with sufficient conviction. The SS made an example
of – what was his name? insisting on total discipline,
or terror, right to the end. I carry the can.

*

Robert Staffin, *1882–1949, was Deputy Works Manager at Daimler-Benz, Mannheim. Staffin had worked as an engineer for Daimler-Benz since 1911. As he stated at the preliminary proceedings conducted by the American authorities in 1946, he was responsible, among other things, for counter-intelligence, including suspected sabotage. An alternative, in the case of Marian Krainski would have been to deal with the matter internally. But almost no thought appears to have been given in general to the well-being of the company's Polish work-force. Although conditions were often worse at outlying subsidiary camps such as Sandhofen (which came under Natzweiler) than at the main camps, almost unbelievably little money was spent either by Daimler-Benz or the SS on the forced labourers they had transported from Dachau, who received 100–120 grams of bread and two bowls of watery soup per day. In Dachau they had been issued with the standard set of KZ clothing for summer, but at Sandhofen there was nothing extra for the winter. They were accommodated so inadequately that their health was in some cases chronically and in others fatally affected. Bronchitis, swollen limbs, swollen and wounded feet (from their wooden shoes), abscesses and vermin-related growths or tumours were all endemic. Some prisoners lost up to half of their normal weight before the last of them left in March 1945. The perverse folly or "craziness of Nazi economic logic" (Mazower) is clearly evident in the fact that it was forbidden for prisoners even to gather refuse or bits of food which had been dropped, or for German workers to give them any food – which some nevertheless succeeded in doing from time to time. Such supplements to their almost non-existent rations, which amounted to no more than 500 calories a day – "(Let me notice in passing," Primo Levi drily observed in a similar context, "that at least 2,000 calories are needed to survive in a condition of total repose)" – would* *obviously have helped to preserve the prisoners' strength and cost the SS and Daimler-Benz nothing but could lead to beatings so severe as frequently to hinder the victim's ability to continue working. It scarcely needs saying that racial contempt and a cold-blooded business appraisal of forced labourers as dispensable combined to produce this sort of behaviour: "Like Hitler himself, German business never saw them as a scarce or valuable resource, still less as human beings to be nurtured and preserved. Rather they were cheap commodities to be worked until they were worn out" (Mazower). At the 1946 American inquiry, three out of the four German witnesses were unable to remember Krainski's name… Staffin and Platzer were sent for trial in Poland, where Platzer was sentenced to five years imprisonment and Staffin to eight. Staffin died while in prison but Platzer returned to Germany in 1950 and was soon back at work for Daimler-Benz in Untertürkheim.*

(xv)

Filip Müller (1), Sonderkommando, Auschwitz

Until the day he wanted to die, he'd thought
the worst was when they opened the big gas-chambers
and the dead who'd rammed the massive doors dropped out
like blocks of blood-smeared basalt. Again he remembers

the vomit, excrement, blood from ears and noses,
the menstrual blood, small children with skulls crushed
beneath their parents, struggling to escape the gas,
the strong on top. But his eyes fill

to speak again of what seemed even worse:
people from home, Czech Jews on their way,
they'd been told, to work elsewhere, now daring to curse
the SS for lying – clubbed, whipped, forced to flee

till, in the 'undressing room', they stand – sing – cry
the Hatikvah, *and their anthem. His tears swell*
at how they begged him not *to join them and die,*
gassed into silence: "Go out now, live and tell."

(xvi)

Filip Müller (2)

And so he lived – to tell of those who died.
Once, when the flues were blocked, two friends could not
go on re-burying corpses slimy with mud
washed up in the flooded pit – lay down – were shot –

while above, like diavoli neri, *the SS guards stood*
and mocked them. He passed though Hell, but wrote it down
for those who died unjustly, and some who died
of a broken conscience. Others went insane

from doing what he did, seeing what he saw.
The SS employed sheer terror. How then help
the hopeless? Inside those gates, who wanted to hear
the truth? One fellow-labourer, encountering there

a friend's wife, warned her. She panicked and, naked, ran
to the women, then the men. When no one listened,
she started screaming. They flogged her till she told them
who told her, and burned him alive. The dead don't tell.

*

Filip Müller, *1922– , was a member of Jewish forced-labour squads at Auschwitz. A Slovakian Jew, Müller was sent to Auschwitz in April 1942 and remained there, mainly at Birkenau, until the SS abandoned the camp in Jan. 1945. The two largest gas-chambers at Birkenau,* Gaskammer II *and* III, *were both about 250 sq. yards in size and capable of killing 2,000–3,000 people in about fifteen minutes. They were known as the* Leichenkeller, *or 'corpse-cellars'. Müller explains in* Shoah *how the victims, who had been told they were entering the shower-rooms, would rush away from the Zyklon pellets – introduced through shafts from the roof of the gas-chamber – towards the doors and how, as more and more died, the strongest would clamber on the heaps of bodies towards the ceiling, desperate for air… The Jewish* Sonderkommandos *were meant to relieve* *the SS of work and stress, but since their members were 'bearers of secrets'* (Geheimnisträger) *they were liquidated themselves at irregular intervals. Müller survived five such liquidations. When Auschwitz was abandoned on 18 Jan. 1945, the last hundred members of the* Sonderkommando *were evacuated together with the other prisoners to KZ Mauthausen, where the SS intended to kill them, but Müller disappeared in the crowd. In 1979, he published* Eyewitness Auschwitz, *of which Raul Hilberg wrote, "I have been through this book page by page and I am hard put to find any error, any material significant error." Hilberg accordingly uses Müller as a source in* The Destruction of the European Jews. *Claude Lanzmann has written of Müller, "He is the embodiment of impossible witness."*

(xvii)

Brigitte Frank, 'Königin von Polen'

The *Führer* took my side. As if I'd let
Hans Frank divorce me after twenty years!
"Not now, Brigitte," he ordered: "Hans must wait
till after the war." I don't give a toss (he knows)

about their politics, but I could have hugged him
when he took my hand and promised: "He'll change his mind."
Now that's what I call a man, a *Menschenkenner*.
As if I'd leave our castle. "Hans," I told him,

"I've born you five pure-blooded German children.
As if I'm going to let you marry your mistress.
I've fought my way from rags to furs. As if
the richest Jews in Kraków weren't my lackeys!"

I've had, as Queen of Frank-Reich, my share of lovers.
When *Vati* drowned himself, I swore I'd thrive.
Gold, silver, jewels, antiques… Soon we'll go home
to Neuhaus – lead a normal family life.

*

Brigitte Frank, 1895–1959, *was known as the 'Queen of Poland'. Her father, who owned a spinning mill, had got himself into financial difficulty and committed suicide in 1908, leaving five children and his wife to be looked after by the latter's family. Later she often said she had grown up in fear of poverty. As soon as she was old enough, she learned stenography and left home for Berlin where, as a girl with no father, she looked for other men to help her. Thus, even in the 1920s, she succeeded in finding work and in gradually bettering herself. In 1924, she met and married Hans Frank, who was at the start of his career as a lawyer and politician.*

Hans Frank, 1900–1946, was five years younger than his domineering wife. From 1930 on, he was Hitler's lawyer, defending him in over forty cases. In 1939, Hitler appointed him Generalgouverneur *of the biggest segment of occupied Poland. Frank had always suffered from delusions of grandeur (in the Academy of German Law, which he founded in 1933, his picture hung next to Hitler's in every office), and in Poland he applied the so-called* Führerprinzip *(whereby a* Führer *assumed absolute authority with respect to whatever group he was to lead, whose duty it was to obey him) with sound and fury. The pretentious Frank and his uncultivated* Königin *were not popular in higher Nazi circles. Goebbels described the former in his diary as "half-mad" and noted caustically, "Frank does not govern, he rules" – hence, no doubt, the use of* Frank-Reich *(France), among Frank's fellow party-members, to refer to the* Generalgouvernement. *His greatest enemy was, of course, Himmler who, by claiming (with Hitler's support) total responsibility for the Jewish question, was at liberty to ride rough-shod over Frank's authority. This irritated Frank intensely and he paid surprise visits to the death-camps of Belzec, Lublin-Majdanek and even Auschwitz (which was beyond his pale), only to be fobbed off. When he complained to Hitler that he could get no detailed information as to what was going on, Hitler is said to have told him, "You can well imagine that there are executions going on – of insurgents. Apart from that, I do not know anything. Why don't you speak to Heinrich Himmler about it?" In spite of being one of those who could claim not to know, however, Frank was fully involved in the establishment of the Polish ghettos and then in emptying them, as well as in the imprisonment and slaughter of innumerable Polish civilians, as part of the Nazi repression – or attempted extermination – of Polish culture. He closed the universities and plundered the Church, museums and the Polish aristocracy for their art treasures (over which he squabbled with Hermann Göring). He and his wife would tour the ghettos and Brigitte collected an enormous number of valuable items from Jewish businesses and families who hoped that she would help them – which she never did. The Franks appear at length in Curzio Malaparte's* Kaputt*: "[The Queen's] whole face was thrust toward the food heaped on precious Meissen plates, toward the scented wine glittering through Bohemian crystal, and on it, around her nostrils, quivered an expression of insatiable greed, almost of gluttonous rage... Perhaps she was hungry?"*

(xviii)

Dr Samuel Steinberg, Häftling, Krankenhaus Block 21, Auschwitz

The doctors there made notes on their victims, I on them:

1 Sick prisoners who were no longer able to work – who had developed septic feet from their wooden shoes or swollen legs as a result of their poor diet – were examined in groups by a senior consultant and sent to Block 20. There they were told that before entering the sick bay they had to take a shower and be deloused. In fact they were conducted one by one into an examination room where they were pinioned to a chair by one medical orderly while another held his hands across their eyes. A Pole by the name of P. then administered an injection to the heart of 4cc of phenol. The patient died within seconds.

Other injections used were an iodine substitute called Sepso, which took twenty minutes, and even benzene or paraffin.

An estimated 25,000 prisoners died by this method.

2 In Block 21 (the surgical block) the doctors 'practised' their skills. Any Jewish prisoner with stomach pains, for example, could be diagnosed as suffering from ulcers and subjected to the standard operations, whether he in fact had ulcers or not. After the operation, such patients received no appropriate nursing, not even a diet of milk. A few days later they would be selected for the gas-chamber.

The same '*Sonderbehandlung*' (special treatment) awaited the patients of Dr K. This young doctor had qualified as a surgeon in 1943 and was keen to learn all forms of amputation. He operated on cellulitis, for instance, when a simple incision would have sufficed, by amputating the finger, or on a phlegmon of the leg by amputating the leg. All such patients were then unfit for work and certain to be gassed.

3 With the help of camp doctors, the pharmaceutical company Bayer conducted experiments with drugs and medicaments. One hundred and fifty Jewish women, whom the firm bought from the camp authorities, were removed to a building outside the main camp and used for experiments with unknown hormone preparations. During the *post mortem* operations, sections of lung and wind-pipe ganglia were removed and sent to a factory laboratory.

Prisoners with tuberculosis unlucky enough not to have been gassed were also injected with Bayer ampoules. There were further experiments in putting people down with intravenous injections of the anaesthetic Evipan. And, of course, the entirely useless sadism of the likes of Mengele.

4 No doubt for geopolitical reasons, some men were castrated and both men and women sterilized. The sterilization process was still in the development stage but was performed by X-raying the womb or testicles for up to five or six minutes. The young men would then be sent back to work but after several weeks or months recalled to Block 21. After questioning about their sexual needs, wet dreams, digestion, etc., they were compelled to masturbate and the sperm collected. Those unable to masturbate received a finger-massage of the prostate gland, which produced an erection. After a number of sessions the masseurs grew tired of this and took to using a sort of crank, which was inserted in the anus. Three or four turns were enough to produce the required effect. The sperm were then microscopically examined by a bacteriologist to see if they were dead…

I could go on. But turn *that* into four stanzas of poetry, if you will.

*

Dr Samuel Steinberg was a forced-labour medical assistant in Auschwitz from 1942 to 1945. A Parisian Jewish doctor transported to Auschwitz, Steinberg's statements in the text are based on KZ Dokument F321 *(1988) – a corrected and completed translation of* Camps de Concentration. Crimes contre la personne humaine *[Paris, 1945], which was prepared by the French authorities after the war for use by the Nuremberg International Military Tribunal. Steinberg's address is given as "3, rue de Navarre, Paris". No doubt this was one of the "forty thousand apartments" whose systematic looting by the Germans is described with characteristic precision and restraint by W.G. Sebald in* Austerlitz *– together with the uncommunicativeness of the immense new "Babylonian library" on the site of the warehousing complex where the loot was sorted, which Austerlitz feels has been specifically designed to bury what happened. Other than his statements in* KZ Dokument F321 *little seems to be known of Dr Steinberg. Beginning with the so-called 'Doctors' Trial' at Nuremberg, however, much has been discovered in the meantime about some of the horrors which Steinberg mentions and about those who perpetrated them. Although Steinberg only gives his initial, "Dr K.", for example, is identified by Hermann Langbein (in* People in Auschwitz*) as Hans Wilhelm König, a young man who took his profession seriously: "On the other hand, König attempted to learn at the expense of the prisoners". Langbein describes König as otherwise courteous, intelligent, industrious and "not inhuman with regard to details". But "when he was no longer interested in the course of the disease, he sent his patient to the gas chamber".*

As for "the likes of Mengele", Dr Josef Mengele conducted painful examinations and sometimes multiple operations – many of them patently nonsensical – on twins and other children, with the aim of demonstrating racial characteristics. Mengele – like many other prominent Nazis, a man of ruthless personal ambition but no great ability – did not hesitate to kill such children if this suited his purpose. One notorious experiment involved dripping aggressive chemicals into children's eyes in order to change their colour to the 'ideal' Aryan blue.

The doctors at Auschwitz and other concentration camps were primarily supposed to attend to the medical needs of the SS. However, it soon became clear that such camps afforded unique conditions for medical research, in the pursuit of which the doctors were enthusiastically supported by Himmler, who in a letter to the egregious Dr Rascher of Dachau "personally assumed the responsibility for supplying asocial individuals and criminals who deserve only to die for [your] experiments" (this was one of the many letters signed in fact by Rudolf Brandt, Himmler's adjutant – see (i)). Rascher's field of investigation was into the effects of air pressure and lack of oxygen at high altitudes on behalf of the Luftwaffe. *Many of his human guinea pigs died in unbearable pain as a result of experiments of almost incredible cruelty. Likewise with Rascher's experiments regarding the effects of extreme cold, in which he was assisted by two academics from the University of Kiel. A report was drawn up and a conference held on "Medical Questions in Marine and Winter Emergencies", at which, in W.L. Shirer's words, "ninety-five German scientists, including some of the most eminent men in the field, participated, and though the three doctors left no doubt that a good many human beings had been done to death in the experiments, there were no questions put as to this and no protests therefore made." Shirer, who was present at the Nuremberg Trials, summed up this particular "tale of horror" as follows: "Although the 'experiments' were conducted by fewer than two hundred murderous quacks – albeit some of them held eminent posts in the medical world – their criminal work was known to thousands of leading physicians of the Reich, not a single one of whom, so far as the record shows, ever uttered the slightest public protest."*

(xix)

Joel Brand, Jewish Rescue Committee, Budapest

After three years of going through the motions,
the foot-dragging caution, the diplomatic gestures
of bureaucrats, of politicians – while
how many suffered and died without help? –

here was a chance, or so it seemed,
to save some lives: "I am willing to sell you," Eichmann told me,
"a million Jews. Goods for blood – blood for goods…
We need 10,000 trucks: one truck, a hundred Jews.

"You can do this deal in Turkey. And tell the Allies
the trucks are only for the Eastern front.
100,000 Jews will wait at the border:
1,000 trucks, and they cross it." – And then? No visa

for Istanbul. No Weizmann, no Shertok – only
in British-occupied Syria. In Syria, no action –
only questions. No deals with the enemy. No
way back but on to Cairo. No help. No million.

*

Joel Brand, *1906–1964, was a founder with fellow-Zionists of the Jewish Aid and Rescue Committee, Budapest. The fate of the Jews was becoming clearer to the outside world as early as 1941, although many treated the reports with scepticism if not incredulity. Eichmann's offer of a million Jews for 100,000 trucks was made to Joel Brand in Budapest in April/May 1944. At his trial, Eichmann admitted to competing with other SS factions to negotiate for Jewish property or influence. He was surprised when Himmler (who was not only short of trucks but had reasons of his own, by this stage, for making contact with the Allies) agreed to his plan, and he went ahead with it.*

Other than mistrust of the SS and an unwillingness to negotiate with Hitler's Germany, one of the main stumbling blocks to helping the Jews was, as the British Foreign Secretary Anthony Eden bluntly put it, "Turkey does not want any more of your people." Nor did the British or the Americans want any more of Brand's people, and impenetrable bureaucratic barriers and reasons of diplomacy were placed in the way of undertaking almost anything to stop or even limit the catastrophe.

For the Jewish Rescue Committee, Eichmann's offer was too tempting to ignore. When the committee telegraphed Istanbul, they received the reply, "Joel should come, Chaim will be there", which they misunderstood to mean Chaim Weizmann, President of the World Zionist Organization. In fact, the telegraph referred to Chaim Barlasz, head of the Jewish Agency in Istanbul, who was then unable to obtain a visa for Brand. Nor could Moshe Shertok, head of the Political Department of the Jewish Agency in Palestine, obtain a visa to come and meet him, but flew to Syria instead. After fifteen wasted days in Istanbul, during which the Hungarian Jews were being transported to the Nazi killing centres at the rate of 12,000 a day, Brand went to Aleppo, where he met Shertok and the British, who flew him to Cairo for exhaustive intelligence interrogations. In Cairo, the British declined to let him go. On one occasion, at the British-Egyptian Club, Brand was addressed by a man who did not introduce himself: "But

Mr Brand," said this stranger, "what can I do with your million Jews? Where can I put them?" Brand later claimed that this was Lord Moyne, the British Minister Resident in the Middle East and a close friend of Winston Churchill's. But, whoever his questioner was, the question itself was no longer relevant: most of Hungary's Jews by that time were dead.

(xx)

Henek, Kinderblockkapo, Auschwitz-Birkenau

As children's *Kapo*, I was forced to select
these for the doctors, those for the gas-chamber,
and did what I could to save a few for 'work'...
When *Ivan* came the Krauts shot all they could find.

Hurbinek is three. His little legs are crippled.
He couldn't talk, but with his furious eyes
begged me to hide him. The sick-bay was abandoned
to the dead and almost dead. But there's an oven.

Perhaps when I get home I'll become a policeman.
The SS had food. The unopened tins I've found
are under Primo's bunk, while I hunt for more.
He's good and doesn't like to steal or kill.

My father and I went out to shoot Romanians
in the woods near our farm. I've learned, and so has Hurbinek,
to use what there is: food, warmth, the Polish nurses.
He wants to learn a *word* before he dies.

*

Henek, *1929 – ?, was a Hungarian youth who became Children's Block Kapo in Auschwitz. The other members of his family had been gassed on arrival. Primo Levi's presentation (in* The Truce, *ch. 2) of the symbiotic relationship of Henek and Hurbinek is one of his most memorable attempts to set down the unimaginable facts of his war-time experiences – his aim* *being, precisely, to resist and reverse what (in 'The Memory of the Offence' in* The Drowned and the Saved) *he called Nazism's "war against memory, falsification of reality, negation of reality". The reality was that nearly all children who arrived in Auschwitz were gassed as unfit for work together with their mothers or grandmothers. A few, such as Henek, who claimed he was eighteen and a bricklayer whereas he was fourteen and a schoolboy, survived by native wit (Elie Wiesel, who was fifteen, similarly claimed that he was eighteen and a farmer) or because some worker needed an assistant or some* Kapo *a favourite. These, and others not gassed immediately, were the inhabitants of the Children's Block to which Levi refers: when Henek was sent to Birkenau, he told the SS his actual age and became the children's Kapo... Some of the children in Auschwitz failed to qualify even for the gas-chamber. In Langbein's* People in Auschwitz, *Dr Lucie Adelsberger describes them dying gradually of dysentery, their starving bodies covered with scabies, their mouths full of burrowing abscesses which hollowed out their jaws and ate holes in their cheeks in the manner of a cancer. As for Hurbinek, Levi wonders if he had been born in Auschwitz. Until early 1943 pregnant women were automatically gassed; later they were allowed to bear their babies who were then drowned by female SS assistants. However, the occasional secret birth took place and possibly Hurbinek had miraculously survived after the death of his mother. If this were so, as Levi observed, he had never seen a tree. And Auschwitz was all he knew of the human project.*

(xxi)

Norbert Masur, World Jewish Congress (Stockholm)

Delayed by Hitler's birthday, he drove up
at 2 a.m.. Calm and impeccably dressed,
he defended their Jewish policy as thrust upon him,
aggrieved at the outcry which greeted Bergen-Belsen.

The danger now was Russia. To show good will,
a thousand Jewish women in Ravenbrück
could be shipped to Sweden, pending further talks.
A perverse ambition shone in his eagle eye.

But Hitler brought him down with a cry of "*Traitor*":
after the old wolf's death in his lair, no Nazi
would trust him. Nor did Churchill or Roosevelt
ever intend to march in step with Germany.

In the end, we saved seven thousand. The *Reichsführer* fled,
disguised as a private. Stopped at a British checkpoint,
he confessed his name, was searched, and swallowed cyanide.
In twelve mad minutes twelve years of power imploded.

*

Norbert Masur, 1901–1971, was a German Jewish émigré living in Stockholm, who in 1945 was chosen to negotiate on behalf of the World Jewish Congress and the Swedish Foreign Ministry at a secret meeting with Himmler, arranged with the assistance of Himmler's Finnish masseur. The meeting took place in the small hours of 21 April. To counter the bad publicity and "hate propaganda" which had been caused by the Allies' discovery of Bergen-Belsen and Buchenwald, Himmler agreed, after a private consultation with his adjutant, Rudolf Brandt (see (i)), to release at first 1,000 and then more than 7,000 Jewish women inmates of Ravensbrück concentration camp: "They were the lucky ones. In Ravensbrück itself, the site of medical experiments, forced sterilizations and unspeakable acts of sadism, systematic gassing and other killing had been going on for several months" (Mazower). Siemens had been one of the main employers of camp labour. But by early 1945 Ravensbrück had become almost as overcrowded and chaotic as Bergen-Belsen with arrivals from Auschwitz and other camps to the east. Under these circumstances, Himmler could easily have released more, but possibly the political embarrassment caused by Eichmann's million (see (xix)) held him back. Altogether about 90,000 died in Ravensbrück, many of them in the final weeks before the camp was liberated by the Red Army... In his 'Report to the WJC', Masur recorded his surprise at the absence of any personal passion in Himmler regarding the Jews. Himmler claimed always to have favoured expulsion but the world had refused to accept more Jewish refugees. The crematoria were solely a health and security measure, he insisted: "The treatment in the camps was severe but just." One gets the impression from Masur's report that Himmler believed his own lies – or some of them.

Only two days later Himmler was in Lübeck to meet the head of the Swedish Red Cross, Count Bernadotte, in the Swedish Consulate. At this meeting Himmler asked Bernadotte to communicate to Eisenhower Germany's willingness to surrender to the West on condition that they continue the war together against Russia. Hitler heard of Himmler's betrayal on 28 April via a Reuter dispatch from Stockholm. Göring as well as Himmler had hoped to rule the Reich after Hitler, and Göring had dared in a telegram from Berchtesgaden, also on 23 April, to suggest that Hitler honour his decree of 29 June 1941 to the effect that Göring should take over as his deputy in case of the Führer's *incapacitation. Hitler declared both of them traitors. Göring, to his astonishment, was arrested by the SS before dawn the next day. In his political testament of 29 April, Hitler appointed Admiral Dönitz as his successor and expelled Himmler from the party and all his state offices. Although Roosevelt had died on 13 April, this made no difference to the Allies' policy of unconditional surrender, and Himmler's diplomatic overtures came to nothing.*

vi

Stephanskirchen (2)

"The Nazis entered this war under the rather childish delusion that they were going to bomb everyone else, and nobody was going to bomb them… They sowed the wind and now they are going to reap the whirlwind."
                                        Sir Arthur 'Bomber' Harris

Although he thought he'd reap what *he* deserved –
An unfulfilling, unfulfilled, dull life –
He'd found the observer too could be observed,
Unfettered, undefeated, like his wife…

*

One hot September Sunday they returned
To Stephanskirchen where, three years before,
They'd first stood in the church which, bombed and burned,
Had been restored, to mark the end of the war.

– But, leaving home, a phonecall. Her best friend
Had suddenly died. Of cancer. The previous week
They'd thought that she was finally on the mend
After her operation, though still weak.

She'd sat and cried. But then, "Let's go," she said –
"And be back in time for the funeral. She wouldn't have wanted
Us only to mourn for her. Although she's dead,
Her wish to be free from pain has, actually, been granted…"

– Which led to something new. He picked brown leaves
Out of her hair. After a woodland swim
She'd pulled him down on top of her. Sex grieves
With dark *élan*. And, darkly, overcame

Her old reluctance to make love outside…
A second time, when they emerged from the wood,
Some road-workers mocked them. But she flushed with pride
To do it at her age. And that it was good

To lie in last year's warm dry leaves. This year's
Were golden or, still fresh, too green to fall.
Her eyes were bright, impulsive, washed by tears
Of mingled joy and sorrow. But *Death takes all*,

Or *Life and death both come from God*, the graves
Beside the church remind them. Over the wall
Behind the graves, with branches full of leaves
And dark-blue fruit, three plum-trees rise and fall

Gravidly, while a woman wielding a pole
Relieves them of their weight. Her three-year-old daughter
Puts the ripe plums in baskets. Church-bells toll –
For whom? for what? For Sunday. The child's laughter

And high-pitched squealing pipe a brief descant as
Old Rumpelstiltskin opens the huge church-door
And grabs her – greets, though fails to recognize
The strangers – grins, and sets her down once more

Beside her mother, who addresses him
As *Opa*. Off he plods then over the fields –
First casting a curious, sidelong squint at them
In half-remembrance – to where their light-green yields

To dark-green sombre woods of close-set pines,
Between which he and his large basket vanish
In search of mushrooms, berries for thick sweet 'wines'
And home-made schnapps… Abruptly the bells finish

Their chorus. Silence fills the mellow air.
Here fat kine give rich milk, bees pine-green honey,
As now they picnic by the stone block's prayer
For peace in our time: "Just give them sufficient money

To keep them happy, Lord. Let them spin gold
From all the fresh or filthy straw they can find…
And let them keep this peace which is as old
As we are. But won't last. I've changed my mind

About how much or little one could do:
Instead of working for the enemy
And justifying our lives as going to show
How little choice we have, the mind is free

To choose, or not to choose – no matter what.
Like Jandl, Caspar Brandner, Norbert Masur,
And poor Joel Brand or Henek, each need not
Think herd- or swarm-thoughts – can always ask, *What for?*

'Others may join the Party. But not I,'
One teacher taught. And not even Himmler threw
Every non-Nazi in Dachau. *Let live* – not *die* –
Was what he meant. But most joined in, it's true,

While many (like me) kept making compromises.
Exile and cunning helped some few survive.
With no real knowledge of what freedom *is*,
In the fight to save it millions lost their lives…

We've had it easy: pampered, unprepared
For hardships which, then, only time resolves,
What do we *know* of those who had it hard –
Broke down – went mad – killed others – killed themselves?…

Two hundred years ago Wordsworth still thought
'The Happy Warrior' – facing blood, fear, pain –
Empowered within, transmuted as he fought
Miserable necessity to glorious gain.

Our civilization only came of age
Later – in that the gutter had not yet
Become the mainstream. In order now to wage
Our wars, we *must* deceive ourselves, forget…

As Rumpelstiltskin has forgotten us
Already. Or, perhaps, he pretended to.
Why risk another discussion? His story has
Changed with my changing mind, as stories do.

The chances are he lived by exploiting others –
Like Walter Stier or Suchomel, survived
Because they died. The youngest of three brothers
In any *Märchen* got back home and thrived…

Upright, well-trained, hard-working, smart, no doubt
His sort fought bravely back – gave rich and poor
The *Wirtschaftswunder*. But when they found out
Who Rumpelstiltskin *was*, he lost his power

And tore himself apart in a mad rage – "
"Like Hitler?"
              "And like Goebbels, Himmler, Göring,
And thousands, it seems, of others. In that age
Of *Führers* big and small – uniform-wearing

Duces and *Conducators*, *Póglovniks* –
Who sought to exploit both lower and upper classes,
Subordinates *and* superiors, poor and rich,

Seducing individual minds *and* masses –

What was it that was new? *'A living thing'* –
To own a living thing – *'is more to me*
Than all the gold or power to which the king
And his father-in-law, the miller, bend the knee':

Materialistic, proud, successful men,
So trodden down and so dehumanized
Their deepest pleasure was to rise again
Like gods – or wanton boys tormenting flies.

Succumbing, in the end, to the futile passion
Or *rage* to own – control or subjugate –
Other men's lives, each in his own mad fashion
Imploded with self-destructive male self-hate…"

– "Who *was* he then?"
 "A loser. Like all who rage
To win, even *if* he'd won, he'd still have lost:
'What shall it profit a man…?' But in our age
We think the world we gain is worth the cost."

– "They also lost the war. Let's go inside
And light black candles in St Stephen's name
For those who died in the fighting – and H. who died
Last night." In the cool church, the undying flame

Hung dimly above a colourful surprise:
The altar rails and steps were decorated
For *Erntedank*. *"One generation dies,*
Another is new born" – he quietly translated

The text on a plain and simple *Sterbebild*,
Set in a bright display of fruit and flowers,
For a wife who'd died in childbirth. Again tears filled
Her swollen eyes, as they had done for hours

Already on that sadly sunny day,

And overflowed on apples, pears, grapes, hops
Twined round a bundle of sweet-smelling hay,
Dahlias, late sunflowers, roses, sweet-corn cobs.

Beside them, German radishes, huge krauts,
Potatoes, carrots, pumpkins, swedes, kohlrabi,
Sheaves of ripe grain – wheat, barley, rye and oats.
And in their midst a photo of the baby.

She crossed herself: "She'll get to know her mother
From others' memories."
      "And that's not to say
That she won't know her, though she'll only gather
As much of the truth as she, her father, or they

Can 'resurrect' – "
     "Like us, then."
         "Let's go up
To the organ loft" – whose rich and civilized view
Through the south windows pans out from the top
Of the church's low green hill, beneath the blue

And blinding white of Chiemgau's surreal sky,
Across the region's smaller lakes to the shore
Of the great lake whose busy motorway
Was built by Hitler, who planned many more

Into the heart of Poland, Ukraine, Russia:
"These windows, perhaps, were smashed five months *before*
The church was bombed: the earth here quaked and pressure
Waves burst through doors, broke glass, when the air war

Hit Munich – "
     "Over fifty miles away?" –
"It seems 131 towns and cities
Were bombed – some once, but many others day
And night – igniting fire-storms – shrivelling pity.

The plain black cross above their prayer for PEACE

IN OUR TIME is like an aeroplane, and no wonder:
The first time we were here, though, the truth is
I'd hardly heard of 'Operation Thunder-

Clap', for example. Or 'Operation Gomorrah'.
Or all their other oh-so-creative names
Encoding more than a million tons of terror
Dropped on 3.5 million German homes

And other targets. To calm my mind, I started
My own 'synoptic, artificial view'
(As W.G. Sebald says) to be read out
Here now, in memory of these things, to you

As German – by myself as English, though
Belonging nowhere, or in *Niemandsland*,
As I have come to see it. Take a pew,
And try to listen – not to understand:

Out of Niemandsland

After the worst inferno their 'block-busters'
And fire-bombs ever ignited – the Battle of Hamburg –
No battle but mass-murder – 42,000
People not gassed but blown up, burnt

To ashes or, in pools of their own fat,
To shrunken brown or purple joints, some stuck
In molten asphalt (feet first, and then hands)
Which, bubbling thickly, trapped and literally roasted

Its victims when it went on fire and blazed –
As water, melting glass, heaped rubble blazed –
In Bomber Command's most hugely successful bonfire,
The likes of which had never before been seen

By human eyes, a two-mile high tornado
Created in fifteen minutes, which roared for three hours
With winds of 150 mph

Sweeping up people like dry leaves, consuming

All oxygen, uprooting trees and flinging
Great chunks of burning wood, roofs, gables, beams,
Bill-boards and dust-bins, fences and garden-gates
Up and away, while thousands died in cellars

Or air-raid shelters, baked or asphyxiated
As 250,000 dwellings, or more
Than half of those in the city, collapsed and burned
Above their heads. After the chaotic flight

Of more than a million people, dumb-struck with terror,
With shocked incomprehension – old men, old women,
Families with children, shop-girls, harbour whores,
Heading for nowhere, carrying almost nothing,

So suddenly had the Feuersturm *come upon them:*
And the Lord rained upon Sodom and upon Gomorrah
Brimstone and fire from the Lord out of heaven;
And he overthrew those cities and all the plain

And all the inhabitants of those cities… and, lo,
The smoke of the country went up as the smoke of a furnace
Of over 1,000 degrees. And its smoke went up
To 20,000 feet and formed a huge anvil.

After that worst of many such infernos –
From Aachen, Braunschweig, Brunswick, Darmstadt, Frankfurt
To Fürth and Halberstadt, Heilbronn and Kassel –
From Köln to Nürnberg, Pforzheim, Wuppertal, Würzburg –

All old and beautiful cities, all destroyed
By fire and brimstone. After that worst came worse."

– "Go on."
        "I got no further."
                "Tell me then."
– "'The Ultimate of Talk'?…"

"What you remember."

– "The war was over. At Yalta Churchill offered
To ease the Russian army's rapid advance
By bombing eastern cities. Dresden suffered,
Perhaps, the most – partly, no doubt, by chance

In that the weather, as at Hamburg, favoured
An all-cremating firestorm, but mainly by
Accurate bombing. Sebald thought Harris savoured
The reek of such destruction personally,

As Hitler fought his personal *Total War*
To subjugate, control – or *own* – men's lives:
When heroes like Churchill lead, who asks *What for?*
(Some asked, I know.) Or when a nation strives

Against another, which of us now would see
Or say, as Joyce did: *'You die for your country, suppose.
But I say let my country die for me'* –
Or add, *'Damn death'* and *'Long live life!'*? Who knows

How he'd react? Words fail us. Who can tell
Even the things we tell ourselves we know,
Which bred word-monsters – *blitz, dehousing, fire-gel,
Strategic bombing, fire-storm*…? Catch 22

Was *LMF*: morality lacked fibre,
As madness wasn't really (was it?) mad.
Some who survived then double-bound their children
Who, later, *wrong if they didn't / wrong if they did*,

Went mad in other ways – or else grew rich.
But that's another story. Dresden was not
A threat. That 'large and splendid' *Florenz*, which
Was crammed with beautiful buildings, works of art,

Helpless civilians, refugees, was attacked
In a massive double-strike by Bomber Command

Three months before the end. If the Brits lacked
The moral fibre to tie Harris's hands,

The Americans followed suit. The result was a raid
To make one feel ashamed of being human.
The first 900 tons of bombs were dropped
On less than four square miles of city centre

At 10.15 pm. The fire-storm started
At once. Some choked in cellars, others burned
Outside them. The *Volkssturm* fought the fires – old men
And boys. Their hopeless task was interrupted

At 1 am, when thousands trying to escape
Were trapped by the next 1,800 tons
Dropped from the second wave of heavy bombers
Into and also around the raging fire-storm –

Already visible hundreds of miles away –
So as to extend it. Blow after blow, explosion
After immense explosion, until no one
Had any idea any longer what was happening.

In the cellars, panicking crowds broke through
Emergency exit walls, crashing from one
Burning, collapsing, smoke-filled hole to the next
To die in piles at the end of city blocks.

Some prayed to God in groups, who hadn't prayed
Since they were children. Others screamed, went mad.
Doors, walls blew in. One woman with three children
Slashed her wrists. One small boy barked like a dog.

Outside the fire grew higher, stronger, hotter.
Thousands were burned or buried under rubble,
Thousands fled to the Elbe. The following morning
Charred bodies lay among the ruined buildings

Like beams of charcoal. With hardly a street discernible,

The *Altstadt* was one huge mound of smouldering débris
And constantly collapsing walls. Survivors searched
For families, friends, possessions. By mid-day

The ruins were filled again with people fleeing
From where they'd lived, clutching peculiar belongings,
Some in pyjamas or nightdresses, leading
Children, grandparents, helping the sick or wounded –

When the USAAF arrived. A further
800 tons of bombs were dropped, completing
The devastation. No one could get away:
All they could do was try and control their terror.

Along the Elbe, later, suitcases, rucksacks,
And corpses: babies dead in prams, dead mothers,
Bomb-scattered limbs, heads, feet, disfigured torsos.
All of which started to rot. Workers in gas-masks

Collected what they could and burned the remains
With flame-throwers – in the *Altmarkt*, for example,
Where SS men retreating from Treblinka
Constructed enormous funeral pyres and cremated

At least 7,000. Many or most of the dead
Were neither identified nor properly counted.
Nobody knows how many died – how many
Thousands of refugees had fled to the city

From further east – how many turned to a handful
Of white-hot ash at over 1,000 degrees,
As 'fire-gel' flared and clung – a form of napalm –
And flagstones burned, glass, girders, living people…

Some of whom still survive. One was a girl
Of twenty at the time – whose mother and father,
Both blind from birth, survived in their own cellar,
After persuading her to escape with the rest.

She feels no hatred now but a wordless sorrow
Mingled with guilt and tears of grateful joy.
Expected and expecting to die of her burns,
She lived to see the baroque *Frauenkirche*,

Which stood for two whole days amid the rubble
Before collapsing, rise again, restored.
But mostly we forget – go looking for trouble –
Make war again – as if we'd never warred…"

*

Outside the sun was lower in the sky
Above the country churchyard: "Thomas Gray,
Mindful of death, began his *Elegy*
With how things end: the curfew, the ploughman's day –

Curfew being when all fires were to be out.
'Large was his bounty and his soul sincere',
His own self-portrait claimed. Far from the crowd,
Stoke Poges lacked its madding strife. As here, –

How does it go? – 'beneath that yew-tree's shade,
Tee-tum tee-tum in many a mouldering heap,
Each in his narrow cell for ever laid,
The rude forefathers of the hamlet sleep…

'Let not ambition mock their useful toil,
Their homely joys and destiny obscure;
Nor grandeur hear with a disdainful smile
The short and simple annals of the poor'"…

– "Imagine *we* were dead…"
                              "Beneath two yews –
Here lie an English man and German woman.
He was a lucky poet, she his Muse:
His pen, her rose, now rest in peace where no one

Can see or hear them."
      "Sounds idyllic."
           "Sounds
Ironic?"
  "*'Wo wird einst des Wandermüden
Letzte Ruhestätte sein?'* The sky surrounds
Our bodies here or there. The grave's a midden."

– *"'How you take it'."*
       Just then a supersonic,
Heavy, low-flying, dark-metal, delta-winged jet
Banged through the evening air like a Miltonic
'Fallen or possible' angel.
      "Not done yet

With reaping the harvest of perpetual peace?"
He murmured, as two slower bombers toiled
Across the sky above the threatened trees
And crouching hills. The 'nature we share' felt soiled

With human sound and fury. But not for long:
The woman with large baskets full of plums
Offers them some and smiles. A familiar song
Reaches their deafened ears. Her daughter comes

Slowly along a row of older tombs
Towards them. At the foot of each she stoops
And, parting green-gold leaves or fading blooms,
Drops with a little splash in its stone stoup

Of holy water a coloured pebble she's found,
Then takes it out again, and so moves on
To the next – a fresh, impressive, flower-heaped mound.
Her words are indistinct but go to the tune

Of – what? *"A cuckoo and a donkey met,"*
He hums: *"Twas in the merry month of May…"* –
"Maria," her mother calls. But not done yet
With taking her stone for a swim, she skips away

To the plain black family grave commemorating
Rosa and Franz's fallen sons, where she stows
Her treasure in its dried-up stoup till later –
Hidden beneath a yew-tree's dusky boughs –

And runs to where her mother waits before
Darkness surrounds the rising moon and a star:
"Tra-la-LA, la-la. Tra-la-LA, la-la.
Tra-la-LA, la-LA, la-LA. La-LA."

vii

Mary and Martha (Working for Others)

"… a certain woman named Martha received him into her house.
"And she had a sister called Mary, which also sat at Jesus' feet, and heard his word. But Martha was cumbered about much serving, and came to him, and said, Lord, dost thou not care that my sister hath left me to serve alone? bid her therefore that she help me.
"And Jesus answered and said unto her, Martha, Martha, thou art careful and troubled about many things.
"But one thing is needful: and Mary hath chosen that good part, which shall not be taken away from her."
                    Luke X. 38–42

As for what really happened, "Lord, please tell
My sister to stop working now and sit
Here at your feet with me," I begged him: "She'll
Say I was slothful." I washed and oiled his feet
With my soft fingers. Martha's hands were red
From washing, cleaning, cooking, kneading bread.

"Not all work, Mary, is the sort of work
You did too long," he reproached me, "selling your body
If not your mind. Many, it's true, see work
As domination. Little Caesars. Already
Our world is work-torn, war-torn. And, worse, many

See war as work, power-greedy, drunk on blood-money.

We harm ourselves, harm nature, harm each other
Fighting to gain / regain the upper hand.
Competing to please God, Abel's big brother
First sowed bad blood. Cain tilled the guilty land.
Then he raised cities. More was always better,
Till time and money forged their double fetter.

The day that Satan chose to rise he fell
And Rome was built. His pride, his ruthless greed –
Which he believed were virtues – made a hell
Of heaven. By other choices, others succeed
In living, converting blame or hate to praise,
In less self-punished, more enlightening ways" –

Which was, I think, when Martha interrupted,
Red in the face as well as with red hands…
He asked which part of things, though treasured, corrupted
On earth. – But then affirmed, till Death demands
His due, both parts are good. His own soul's quest
Began in Joseph's workshop, enabling the rest.

And so we went to eat the food she'd prepared:
Fish cooked with olives. He thanked her, saying right work
Dresses and tends the Tree of Life, as shared
By all things mortal. He broke the bread. Hooks lurk
In craving for and clinging to what ought
To help souls free themselves by its support.

To redeem the time, he said, we need to believe
In what we do: lies always sap resolve.
But if one had to lie so as to survive,
Then let him, later, say so. We need to absolve
Ourselves from our 'devices'. Crossed with pride,
Guilt rots or rages, drives to suicide…

And only very rarely need one die
Telling the truth – which Jew and Roman now

Were blind to. The choice was his: we should not cry
Or fast, but live in peace, observing how
He had no human enemy. As the Son
Of Man, he neither lost nor won.

EPILOGUE: RILKE – IN THE SAME RIVER TWICE

i

Turn

"The way from intense awareness to greatness is through sacrifice." – *Kassner*

Long had he triumphed by looking.
Stars would drop to their knees,
Wrestled there by his gazing.
Or, if he knelt to look,
Even the gods grew weary
Breathing his powerful incense;
Smiled at him in their sleep.

Towers he would look at until –
Frightened – they shook;
Building them up again, quickly, in one!
Yet how often the landscape,
Heavy laden with day,
Rested at last in his peaceful awareness, evenings.

Animals, trustful, moved
Into his open gaze,
Grazing. The captive lions
Stared, as at inconceivable freedom.
Birds went flying through him –
Straight through his soul; and flowers
Looked again in his eyes, as
Large as in children.

And rumours that someone was looking
Moved all the less, the
Questionably visible,
Moved the women.

How long looking?
How long inwardly lacking –
Pleading from deep in his eyes?

While he sat waiting, away from home; a hotel's
Distracted, averted bed-room
Sullen around him, and in the evaded mirror
Again the hotel-room
And, later, from the miserable bed
Again:
Consultations held in air,
Incomprehensible consultations –
Over his feeling heart,
Over his heart which in spite of his pain-racked
Body still made itself felt –
Were taking place and deciding:
That it had no love.

(And denied him greater glory.)

For there's a limit, you see, to looking.
And the well-looked-at world
Wishes to flourish in love.

Work of the face is done,
Now do heart-work
On the images captured within you; for you
Overpowered them: but, now, you don't know *them.*
Look, inner Man, at your young inner Woman,
At the one you have won from
A thousand natures, at
The creature you've still only won, the
Never yet loved one.

ii

L'Ange du Méridien

(Chartres)

With all the force of nihilistic thought,
A tempest tests this huge cathedral's strength;
And so it's with a sense of something sought
That we're attracted by your smile at length,

O feeling angel, by your gentle smile
Whose mouth is sculpted from a hundred mouths…
But are you aware – or not – how our life's hours
Slip from the fullness of your dial,

Whose figures show the whole day's total, which,
Equally real, are balanced there as fully
As if all hours were ripe and rich. –

What do you, stone one, know of our Being's plight,
Turning, perhaps, with deeply, even wholly
Ecstatic looks, your sun-dial towards the night?

ACKNOWLEDGEMENTS AND NOTES

The poems and translations in this book are both a work in their own right and a further selection from *Then and Now – Opus 3*. Some of them first appeared in the following magazines: *Acumen, Agenda, Areté, HQ Magazine, Long Poem Magazine, Metre, Modern Poetry in Translation, Pennine Platform, Poetry Review, Poetry Wales, The Shop, The Warwick Review*. *Working for the Enemy* and an earlier version of *after jandl* were included in the first selection from *Opus 3, Boccaccio in Florence and Other Poems* (2009), and here take their proper places in *Self-Portrait as a White-Collar Worker (4) – Afterwords*. The *Prologue* and *Epilogue* were also included in *Boccaccio in Florence*. The translations (and, in some cases, imitations) of poems by Ernst Jandl are published by kind permission of Luchterhand Literaturverlag.

A brief note on the following notes may be of use, particularly since some are of an unfamiliar variety – consisting of essay-like commentary as much as if not more than background information. One reason for this is that where verse seemed inappropriate to some of the subject-matter of this book I have used the (generally) more straightforward medium of prose – and not only in the notes – rather than not say what needed saying. In this as in other respects the book as a whole has been influenced by the extraordinary, genre-crossing – in effect, genre-*querying* – writings of W.G. Sebald (Wertach in Allgäu, 1944–2001, Norwich). *Afterwords* has been written, even so, to be read like any other annotated edition, i.e. the main text first (and second or third), since this can practically be understood without the notes, which then add to it. After the notes, ideally, the relevant section(s) of main text again. And so on.

p.3 "**Enough! or Too much**": As noted in *Boccaccio in Florence and Other Poems*, *The Curse* virtually reverses the meaning of Blake's dictum in *The Marriage of Heaven and Hell*, where it implies that "The road of excess leads to the palace of wisdom."

p.5 *The Carpenter's* **Cook's Tale. Or:** *Blindman's Buff*: The opening lines of *Blindman's Buff* have been approximately taken over (by the Master Carpenter who turns out to be telling the story) from Chaucer's unfinished *Cook's Tale*. Chaucer's own Carpenter is one of a group of five guildsmen not allotted a tale in *The Canterbury Tales*. Of these guildsmen no more is known than the few lines devoted to their "*fraternitee*" in *The General Prologue*. They have brought with them on the pilgrimage a ribald and somewhat unappetizing Cook (suffering from a dry scabbed ulcer on his shin) who is inspired by the scurrilous humour of *The Reeve's Tale* – "*Ha! ha! quod he, for Christes passion, / This millere hadde a sharpe conclusion…*" – to tell one of his own… Chaucer's idea was that his thirty pilgrims should tell two tales on the way to Canterbury and two coming back, but only about a fifth of these had been written by his death or disappearance some time after 5 June, 1400 – the last known reference to him as still alive. In the case of *The Cook's Tale*, Chaucer may, of course, have intended to complete or rewrite what he had started. However, the Cook himself introduces it as "*a litel jape that fil in oure citee*", and if it was in fact the case that Chaucer had some such Boccaccian tale as *Decameron* IX,v – on which *Blindman's Buff* is very loosely based – in mind for the Cook, he may well have abandoned it as too similar in theme (a rather heartless practical joke or revenge story) to *The Miller's Tale* and *The Reeve's Tale* which precede it. In any case, the Master Carpenter is no "*cherl*" – as Chaucer evidently thought the Cook was – and is here presented as turning the "*litel jape*" into more than a "*cherl's tale*". He is also presented as a friend of Chaucer's and as picking up the threads of the latter's *Cook's Tale* ten years or so after his disappearance, around the time that Henry IV had become so ill – some said as a punishment for murdering Richard II – that he had been compelled to leave the day-to-day government of the country to the future Henry V and had retired to Lambeth Palace where his comrade-in-arms, Thomas Arundel, whom the Carpenter believes to have been Chaucer's arch-enemy, was still Archbishop… But, of course, the tale – like those of Boccaccio and Chaucer himself – is fiction rather than history and takes anachronistic and other liberties of the imagination with whatever really happened.

p.5 "*Ella, rispondogli, cominciò a guatare…*": "She, having returned his greeting, began to gaze at him…" In Boccacio's tale, Calendrino – the "*modesto pittore*" (as Vasari called him) who is the butt of several other practical jokes in *The Decameron* – falls in love, while working on the frescoes at Camerata, near Florence, with a girl who turns out to be a local prostitute. His colleagues, Bruno and Buffalmacco (cp. *The Chest* in *Boccaccio in Florence*), first of all encourage Calendrino's infatuation and then arrange to have his wife, Tessa, catch him with the girl *in flagrante delicto*. Monna Tessa's furious onslaught leaves Calendrino badly scratched, torn and bleeding, and she drags him off home to Florence with his tail between his legs – where, to the great amusement of his friends, he is vexed and humiliated day and night ("*il dì e la notte molestato ed afflitto*") by his wife's reproaches.

p.6 **before he'd fully served / his time**: Apprenticeships lasted seven years – which explains, if it does not excuse, the virulence of Perkin's later desire to pay his master back.

p.7 **Buridan – / first loved, then dumped, in Paris by Queen Jeanne**: Cp. Villon's famous *Ballade*, translated in *Two Extracts from* The Testament (p.27). Queen Jeanne of Navarre was a fourteenth century French queen who was reputed to have had her lovers, after three days of merry-making, tied up in a sack and thrown out of her window into the Seine. The story may or may not be apocryphal according to which the philosopher Buridan was subjected to this treatment while a student but survived by arranging to have a barge full of hay float past the window at the critical moment. Rigoletto's attempt to assassinate his daughter's violator goes wrong in another way, of course…

p.8 **the Boar's Head**: The famous hostelry of *Henry IV* Pts 1 and 2, which take place around the time of Chaucer's death, may not in fact have existed until later. However, the Carpenter follows – or should one say *precedes*? – the illustrious example of Shakespeare by situating it in Eastcheap around 1400. As for the **Garter** (p.8), the 1971 Arden edition of *The Merry Wives of Windsor* asserts, without quoting its authority, that "There was apparently a real Garter Inn at Windsor in the sixteenth century". Of course, the action of Shakespeare's play (very possibly written *between* the two parts of *Henry IV*) is set – or, rather, set as well – at the beginning of the *fifteenth* century. Or how could Falstaff appear in it at all or Master Fenton have "kept company with the wild prince and Poins" (III.ii.66), for example?

p.15 *"My sone, keep wel thy tonge"*: The Carpenter is here quoting from one of Chaucer's fables, *The Manciple's Tale*, in which Mercury's pet crow tells tales on his master's unfaithful wife, as a result of which he kills her. Of course, he then hates and punishes the crow…

p.20 **Chaucer – for he it was**: Some of the details of *The Carpenter's* Cook's Tale from this point on are derived from F.N. Robinson's edition of *The Works of Geoffrey Chaucer* (1933, 1957) – to which everyone who reads Chaucer is indebted. Robinson notes the curious anomaly that "far from giving any information about his literary work, contemporary documents do not once betray the fact that he was a man of letters". A number of more recent scholars have drawn attention as well to how little we know of the last year or more of Chaucer's life, after the accession of Henry IV in September 1399. Chaucer seems to have died some time between 5 June 1400 and, possibly, 1402, but there is no clear evidence as to how or where; nor did he leave a will, which has been described by a leading historian of the period as puzzling, to say the least, for a man of his standing. On the other hand, there is only circumstantial evidence relating to the death of King Richard himself... Perhaps not very surprisingly, deciphering or uncovering who said and did what seems to be no easier when it comes to medieval England than with more recent falsifiers of history – see *Self-Portrait as a White-Collar Worker (4)*. Some historians (as in T. Jones *et al.*, *Who Murdered Chaucer?*, 2003) now take the view that the traditional version of events, according to which Henry Bolingbroke, wishing to do no more than reclaim his inheritance, felt obliged to relieve the country of an unpopular, incompetent, morally flawed and foolish Richard, was largely the (intended) result of Lancastrian propaganda and/or pressure – as were contemporary chroniclers' descriptions of the usurpation as a bloodless revolution. As everyone knows from Shakespeare, Henry was Richard's cousin and had grown up amid the extraordinary political tensions of Richard's minority before getting himself exiled in 1398 because of his mysterious – and still unexplained – quarrel with Thomas Mowbray. His return from exile in 1399 may in fact have been more of a calculated and ruthless political *coup* than Shakespeare had any way of knowing. According to this hypothesis, at least some of the calculation stemmed from the former Archbishop of Canterbury, Thomas Arundel, whom Richard had exiled for treason in 1397 and who could easily have planned the deposition in Paris together with Henry. Arundel, at any rate, returned with Henry's party and marched with them through England, bribing and threatening others to join the rebellion. He at once reinstated himself as Archbishop of Canterbury, in defiance of the Pope as well as Richard... For Shakespeare's historically somewhat inaccurate but nevertheless brilliantly perceptive view of the period which included the last few years of Chaucer's life, one has only to turn to his sequence of five plays: *Richard II*, *1 Henry IV*, *The Merry Wives of Windsor*, *2 Henry IV* and *Henry V*. Interestingly, Shakespeare seems to have been almost as antipathetic towards Henry IV as are modern historians. If his attitude towards Richard is more ambivalent, he presents both kings as the slaves of history (the oxymoron is Tolstoy's) – deceiving themselves, as well as others, in different ways. Shakespeare quite clearly saw the deposition not only as a catastrophe in itself but as setting off a whole chain of catastrophic events... *The Carpenter's* Cook's Tale alludes as well to *Measure for Measure*, whose plot involves similar elements. The fall and redemption of Angelo (as one may think of it) is remarkable for taking place in a Vienna peopled largely by Londoners, including a descendant of the Carpenter's 'Pompey' – whose real-life equivalent no one will convince me Shakespeare had not encountered at the Boar's Head in Eastcheap.

p.20 **Retractions**: As F.N. Robinson says, there are many instances more or less parallel to Chaucer's "*retracciouns*", and he provides a short list, from St Augustine to Tolstoy, which "might easily be extended". Apart from this obviously ancient literary convention, there was also something of a rash of religious recantations – particularly by Oxford intellectuals – around 1400, relating to the (heretical) teachings of John Wyclif and the spread of Lollardy. Archbishops Courtenay and then Arundel, in particular, were keen on getting both Church and laity back in line – and it has been suggested that Chaucer's retractions together with his thoroughly orthodox *Parson's Tale* (a sermon in prose on Confession and the Seven Deadly Sins) were written under duress.

p.21 "*he was a good felawe, etc.*": This passage from the *General Prologue*, describing the Shipman, is here applied by the Carpenter to the "former smuggler", Pompey.

p.21 **what Henry was up to**: There is no way of knowing, of course, exactly when Bolingbroke – with or without the support of Arundel – started thinking about a *coup*, but the peace-loving Richard, who modelled his relatively enlightened Renaissance court on such as Robert of Anjou's, where Boccaccio had spent his youth, had long been unpopular with his war-mongering barons. To make matters worse, some of the more prominent of these had exercised unusual power (while squabbling over it among themselves) between Richard's accession in 1377 and his coming of age in 1389. Henry's humorless and vindictive mind may in fact have been mulling a rebellion over for some time before his actual exile… But whatever his thoughts were, his consequent usurpation and regicide provided, needless to say, sufficiently dramatic raw material for Shakespeare's subtle portrayal of this particular revenger's tragedy. Possibly all tyrants are soft-centred and/or mad: hence their indomitable and self-destructive need to assert their authority. At any rate – as Henry almost confesses in Shakespeare's play – uneasy lay the head that stole Dikkon's crown.

p.21 **I'd worked on Chester quire**: The carving of the stalls in Chester cathedral dates from around 1380 and is considered some of the finest medieval woodwork in Europe. As full of devils as it is of angels, this delicate but not cheerful piece of work has been likened to an enormous crown of soaring thorns. As for the Master Carpenter's meeting Chaucer **on the pilgrimage**, the *General Prologue*, as Robinson says, "is usually associated with 1387". However, "There has been much speculation as to what suggested to Chaucer the idea of a pilgrimage. He may, of course, have been describing an actual experience, or more than one": i.e. the pilgrimage on which the Carpenter and Chaucer met is here imagined as dating from not long after the completion of Chester quire.

p.22 **not least by knocking clerics in his rhymes**: Chaucer had also written excellent poems of impeccable piety – such as *The Man of Law's Tale*, *The Clerk's Tale*, *The Prioress's Tale* and *The Second Nun's Tale*. However, these are probably earlier work and not quite so well known even now as *The Pardoner's Prologue*, *The Friar's Prologue* and *Tale*, *The Summoner's Prologue* and *Tale*, *The Shipman's Tale*, *The Canon's Yeoman's Prologue* and *Tale*, in all of which clerics are unforgettably held up as "scroungers, thieves or wealthy hypocrites…".

p.22 **he rented a new place etc.**: This was a fine old tenement and not a bolt-hole. Even so, Chaucer could have claimed whatever protection the sanctuary of Westminster Abbey might have afforded, had he wished to – though there was in fact no guarantee that the King or Arundel would not violate it, as they did on more than one occasion.

p.22 **Free-thinking speech became a thing of the past**: The earlier fourteenth century had in fact been an era of relatively free thought, typified by the proto-Protestant John Wyclif and the Lollards with their radical criticism of the Church's vast wealth and pursuit of political power. While there had always been criticism of the Church from within, one of the reasons for this "crisis of faith", as it has been called, was very possibly the Black Death (cp. *Boccaccio in Florence*, pp. 127–128). Wyclif and the Lollards, at any rate, had been blamed for the Peasants' Revolt of 1381, and the Church had already done battle with Oxford Wycliffe theologians in the 1380s. After the accession of Henry, the freedom to say what one thought came to an abrupt and ruthless end. King Richard had been consistently opposed to the Continental practice of burning heretics and other needlessly cruel or terrifying punishments such as hanging, drawing and quartering. However, the 1401 statute *De Haeretico Comburendo* stated that heretics were to be "burnt before the people in a conspicuous place; that such punishments may strike fear into the minds of others…" And before the law had even been passed, one William Sawtre had the unenviable distinction of being the first Englishman to be burnt in public at Smithfield. "After this terrible example," wrote one chronicler, "other accomplices of his recanted their heresies in person at St Paul's Cross." After Chaucer's death the repression continued, until in 1409 Archbishop Arundel published his *Constitutions*, which have been described as "one of the most draconian pieces of censorship in English history". With all the thoroughness of the Inquisition,

"Every warden, head, or keeper of a college or principal of a hall or hostel", for example, "shall inquire diligently every month at least in the college, hall or hostel over which he presides whether any scholar or inhabitant of any such college, hall or hostel, has held, defended, or in any way proposed any conclusion, proposition, or opinion, sounding ill for the Catholic faith or good customs." And so on.

p.24 *"Ther is namore to say, etc."*: The Carpenter here cuts and pastes assorted passages from *The Canterbury Tales* as if Chaucer had quoted and adapted his own lines in his narration of the painter's story. His main sources are *The Shipman's Tale*, *The Miller's Tale*, *The Reeve's Tale* and the Host's words at the end of *The Pardoner's Tale*.

p.26 **like snails**: Cp. *Decameron* VIII, iii, another story about the painter Calendrino in which he dreams of getting rich quick – "without having to daub walls all the time, like a lot of snails…" The Boccaccian tale which Chaucer couldn't place is, of course, *Decameron* IX, v – "a fine / If heartless story" (*Boccaccio in Florence*, p.51), which might have been expected to appeal to the author of *The Merchant's Tale*, *The Reeve's Tale*, etc. But for all the tough-mindedness of his later writings, Chaucer's sense of compassion (*"For pitee renneth soone in gentil herte"*) was his great step forward – one which, in innumerable forms and variations, Shakespeare himself was later to follow, from *Titus Andronicus* at the very beginning of his career to Prospero's words to Ariel at its end:

> Hast thou, which art but air, a touch, a feeling
> Of their afflictions, and shall not myself,
> One of their kind, that relish all as sharply
> Passion as they, be kindlier moved than thou art?
> Though with their high wrongs I am struck to the quick,
> Yet with my nobler reason 'gainst my fury
> Do I take part: the rarer action is
> In virtue than in vengeance: they being penitent,
> The sole drift of my purpose doth extend
> Not a frown further.

p.27 *Two Extracts from* **The Testament**: Far from leaving no will at all, like his precursor Chaucer, Villon left two: *The Legacy* (1456) and *The Testament* (ca. 1461) – both of them, however, in the medieval form of a mock testament. Although the more substantial of these, *The Testament* (of which ll. 329–356 and ll. 413–532 are translated here) includes the usual jocular and satirical elements, it is also a deeply serious work, notably in its opening section of 832 lines, in which Villon writes on death and 'death's messengers', among other things, as very few poets have ever written – "kindlier moved", to quote Prospero again, with a rare (though also Chaucerian) combination of tough-mindedness and compassion. One reason for this in so young a poet (Villon was born in 1431) may be that he had been closer to death at an early age than most of us are now until we at last begin to deteriorate as 'senior citizens'... Be that as it may, even less is known about Villon's life than about Chaucer's – apart from the fact that he was frequently in trouble. Having spent some years as a student in Paris, he got into a fight with a priest – killed him – was pardoned for the murder – was one of a gang of student-thieves who stole 500 *écus* from the College of Navarre – was imprisoned – pardoned again, but (very possibly because as a known murderer he was more or less unemployable) was soon in trouble again (like the old woman in the *Ballade* which follows the second extract in Villon's original, he might have complained, "I can't get into circulation / Any more than worthless currency"!) until at last, as the result of a street-fight, he was arrested and sentenced to be hanged. At some point amid these vicissitudes, he wrote the famous quatrain:

> My name is François, that's my curse,
> Born in Paris, near Pontoise,
> And from a six-foot cord in a noose
> My neck will feel the weight of my arse.

However, as far as is known, it never came to this. His sentence was commuted, but – "because of the bad way of life of the said Villon" – he was banished from Paris. The year was 1463 and Villon was thirty-two. He seems to have left the city and, like Chaucer, disappeared from history.

p.27 **like a tub of lard**: Another would-be lover tipped into a river was, of course, Falstaff in *The Merry Wives of Windsor* – Falstaff the philosophical, word-making, word-breaking reveller ("What is honour? A word. What is in that word honour? What is that honour? Air." – *1 Henry IV*, V.i.134–135) who, robbed of his booty on Gad's Hill, "lards the lean earth as he walks along", to quote Prince Hal (II.ii.104) – the heir to the throne being fond, as his "fat-witted" friend complains, of "unsavoury similes" (I.ii.2, 77).

p.28 **And won't *I* die, a poor bag-man / From Rennes?** A bag-man or pedlar might also have been (like Autolycus in *The Winter's Tale*) a ballad-monger or poor man's minstrel ("Rennes" presumably refers to one of Villon's absences from Paris). Villon's irony is complex since ballads and other popular songs were often of poor quality, perhaps especially when the ballad-writer had been hired on the cheap to abuse one's enemies – which *The Testament* does. When Hal helps Poins to hide Falstaff's horse on Gad's Hill, Falstaff exclaims, "Hang thyself in thy own heir apparent garters! If I be ta'en, I'll peach for this: and I have not ballads made on you all, and sung to filthy tunes, let a cup of sack be my poison..." (*1 Henry IV*, II.ii.43–46). On the other hand, after his farcical capture of Sir John Colevile of the Dale in Pt 2, Falstaff presents him to Hal's incredulous brother, Prince John, with the words, "I beseech your Grace, let it be booked with the rest of this day's deeds, or by the Lord I will have it in a particular ballad else with my own picture on top on't, Colevile kissing my foot..." (V.iii.61, 44–48). Falstaff's irony is, if anything, more complex than Villon's – nevertheless, he pays more than lip-service to the fact that one of the oldest functions of literature (including, for Falstaff, the Bible) is to ensure that people and events are not forgotten. Needless to say, this seems to have been one of the deepest roots of Villon's poetry – as well as, for example, of Shakespeare's *Sonnets*. At any rate, Villon (like Falstaff, Laura, Pompey, Bolingbroke, even Chaucer himself) is one of the many voluntary and involuntary outsiders – including political *personae non gratae* – whose stories are remembered or recounted in *Afterwords*.

p.28 As long as I've had my fun / I'll rest under any sod: Villon's lines are reminiscent in several ways of the poem by Heinrich Heine now inscribed on his gravestone in Paris and translated in *Heine's Grave* in *Then and Now – Words in the Dark* (p.114): "Sick and tired of life's long journey, / Where at last will I recline?..." At the end of *Heine's Grave*, 'Heine' – who was, of course, an exile *in* as Villon was an exile *from* the city of Paris – recites an English version of his poem *Jetzt Wohin?* (Where to now?), which ends:

> Sadly I inspect the sky
> Where a thousand stars are dozing.
> But among so many I
> Cannot see my own reposing.
>
> Lost perhaps. Astray in heaven's
> Labyrinthine golden mystery.
> Just as I have gone astray
> In the sludge of human history.

At the end of *The Testament*, Villon implies that he was suffering from venereal disease, which may have been the cause as well of the sickness which confined Heine to his *Matratzengruft*, or 'Mattress-grave' (see *Lazarus* in *From Now to Then*). Like Heine, Villon compares his poverty to that of Lazarus in *Luke XVI* – "*C'est de Jhesu la parabolle*" (l.813)... Apparently there is no reference to Villon in Heine's works, but it is hard to imagine that the author of *Vermächtnis* (*From Now to Then*, pp.15–16) was unfamiliar with the more scurrilous and more vindictive sections of *The Legacy* and *The Testament*:

> Now that I can scarcely breathe,
> Like a Christian I bequeathe –
> As befits this hour of truth –
> Jaundiced eye and aching tooth
>
> To my worthy enemies: I,
> Weak of limb but sound of mind,
> Hereby leave my griping wind
> And my grinding poverty
>
> To the rich and greedy. May
> All whose virtues barred my way
> Rot with clap. Acute attacks
> Lay them helpless on their backs.
>
> Etc.

p.33 *by flooding the world and drowning everyone*: Jove justifies this to the other gods by promising

> for to frame a newe,
>   an other kinde of men
> By wondrous meanes, unlike the first,
>   to fill the world agen.

In fact, Deucalion and Pyrrha, who survive "in a little Barke", multiply, to begin with, by throwing over their shoulders the bones of their Grandmother Earth – i.e. rocks and stones – which turn into people. And so the mischief is reincarnate:

> Of these we are the crooked ympes,
>   and stonie race in deede,

>   Bewraying by our toyling life
>   from whence we doe proceede.

Jove later drowned everyone again, except for Baucis and Philemon, the poor peasants who were the only people willing to invite himself and Mercury, disguised as travellers, to stay with them for the night. But as Ovid clearly realized it always would, Jove's new world – since humanity makes its gods in its own image – turned out again to be all too human.

p.34 **Acrisius, Danae's father, etc.**: When Acrisius, king of Argos, consulted an oracle on how to get a son, he was told he would have no sons but that his grandson would kill him. He therefore imprisoned his daughter Danae – who had already been seduced by Acrisius' twin brother, Proetus, builder of the massive walls at Tiryns – in an impregnable tower. When Danae gave birth to Perseus, Acrisius would not believe that Jove was the father but, suspecting his brother again, set his daughter and her child adrift at sea. However, after many heroic and bloody adventures, including the decapitation of Medusa (on whom Jove's brother Neptune had fathered Pegasus) and the rescue of another daughter ill-treated by her father, Andromeda, from Neptune's anger, Perseus was attending a games in honour of a neighbouring king's dead father when his discus was guided by Jove and Acrisius was killed as the oracle foretold.

p.36 **Neptune's lightly trod / The waves**: After claiming the throne of Crete in defiance of his brothers, Minos boasted that the gods would show their approval by answering his first prayer. And sure enough, when he prayed to Neptune for a bull to sacrifice, a beautiful and dazzlingly white specimen emerged from the waves. But Minos was so impressed by this creature that he kept it, and sacrificed another. Neptune was, of course, enraged and, to punish him, made Pasiphae, Minos's wife, fall in love with the bull.

p.36 **Sly Daedalus helped**: Daedalus, the famous Athenian craftsman, was living in exile in Crete after murdering a rival. He helped Pasiphae by constructing a hollow wooden cow in which she could conceal herself. After she had borne the Minotaur, Daedalus also constructed the Labyrinth – thought by some to be the palace at Knossos – in which King Minos spent the rest of his life, imprisoning Pasiphae and the Minotaur at its centre. In fact, as Joseph Brodsky wrote in *Watermark* (1989), "The whole business is, in a manner of speaking, Daedalus' brainchild, the labyrinth especially, as it resembles a brain."

p.36 **Tyndareus**: King of Sparta and Leda's husband. Of the belligerent twins, Castor and Pollux, the latter was an Olympic prize-fighter and could be told from the former by his broken nose, missing teeth, etc. Whether Jove fathered all four children or not, this less than immaculate conception led in the fullness of time not only to the Trojan War but to the Dioscuri's bloody rivalry with the twin sons of Tyndareus' brother, Aphareus, and to all the horrors of the House of Atreus. Or, as W.B. Yeats, two millennia later, more memorably put it:

> A shudder in the loins engenders there
> The broken wall, the burning roof and tower
> And Agamemnon dead.
>   Being so caught up,
> So mastered by the brute blood of the air,
> Did she put on his knowledge with his power
> Before the indifferent beak could let her drop?

p.41 **And their gods cry out and whimper**: The plural in Heine's original ("*Christengötter*" – literally, Christian gods) presumably refers to the Father, the Son, the Holy Ghost and the (in Spain) ubiquitous Virgin – who would constitute more than one god in the eyes of Almansor.

p.42 **a witch's Evil / Eye**: Heine's near-contemporary, Goya (1746–1828) – whose relationship to the 'enlightened' intellectualism of the eighteenth century and to the Romantic attitudes and ideas which succeeded it was as complex as Heine's – also included witches, monsters, metamorphosed animals and the like in his work. Goya's comment on this in a letter to a friend would have appealed to the later Heine: "I am not afraid of witches, nor of poltergeists, ghosts, giants, etc.… I am afraid of no creature but one: man."

p.43 **On the almemor's balustrade**: The almemor is "the pulpit in the centre of the synagogue" (Branscombe). The word is absent from *The Oxford English Dictionary*.

p.44 **Don Jehuda ben Halevy**: Heine, with typical license, changes the name of the great medieval Sephardic poet, Judah ha-Levi (1075–1141), to fit his metre. The beautiful but ambivalent poem, *Jehuda ben Halevy* – a masterpiece of digression and (as "Sometimes in Arabian folk-tales") of digressions within digressions – follows *Prinzessin Sabbath* in *Hebräische Melodien*, throughout which (as J.L. Sammons expresses it) "the complex, antithetical facets of Heine's revived Jewish feeling find expression".

p.45 *Schalet, schöner Götterfunken, etc.*: Heine is, of course, adapting and making fun of Schiller's *Ode to Joy*, schalet (which made it into the *OED Supplement* in 1986) being a delicious Jewish dish of meat and vegetables, traditionally prepared on a Friday for the Sabbath. The opening stanzas from Schiller's undeservedly famous piece of Romantic / Germanic enthusiasm (published in 1786) which were selected by Beethoven for his Ninth Symphony can be translated as follows:

Ode to Joy

> Heavenly Joy, Elysium's daughter,
> Brightest flame of love divine,
> Drunk with drinking your fire-water,
> We approach your holy shrine!
> Re-united with each other,
> Parted souls draw near and marry;
> Each shall be the other's brother
> Where your soft wings waft and tarry.
>
> All who've won a friend for life,
> Or for every situation
> Gained a faithful loving wife,
> Join with us in jubilation!
> Even if only one loved heart
> Has been placed in his safe-keeping!
> Otherwise, let him depart
> From our magic circle, weeping.

Schiller continues:

> Millions, I embrace you all!
> World, I kiss you as a whole!
> Brothers, o'er the stars above us,
> There must dwell a God who loves us.
> Millions, do you bend the knee?
> Can you, World, your Maker see?
> Seek Him o'er the stars above us:
> There a God must dwell who loves us!

It should, perhaps, be emphasized that this is a translation, not a parody...

Heine's joke is good-humoured enough and one hesitates to overload it. Nevertheless, in the context of *Prinz Israel's* exclusion, as though he were a dog, from the so-called brotherhood of man, the lines *"Otherwise, let him depart / From our magic circle, weeping"* take on – however fleetingly – a more ominous shade of meaning. Who or what is to decide, after all, who is to join in the general rejoicing and who not? Who, in other words, is to be designated – and by whom – *persona non grata*? Beethoven's symphonies were, of course, very popular among Nazi audiences, who did not (as W.G. Sebald says in *Air War and Literature*, 1999) "go deeply into the complex question of the relationship between ethics and aesthetics…" The *Führer's* personal favourites were Wagner, Brahms and Bruckner. Thus, "Whenever it seemed advisable to invoke the gravity of the hour a full orchestra was conscripted, and the regime identified itself with the affirmative statement of the symphonic finale"… Later in Schiller's poem there are four lines which were, fortunately, not included in Beethoven's Ninth:

> Weave our sacred circle tightly,
> Swear upon this golden wine;
> Swear to keep our oath divine
> To the One who judges rightly.

The fact that *"Rettung von Tyrannenketten"* (salvation from the chains of tyranny) – Schiller's very next line – can all too easily take on tyrannical aspects of its own is (or should be) clearer now than it was perhaps then. Two hundred years of European history later, Joseph Brodsky – another Jewish *émigré*, this time from Russia – wrote of the inherent danger in the modern world of large-scale political, social or religious groups (all of which have their own literatures, music and other art-forms) and thus of the importance of thinking and acting as an individual rather than thinking and doing what one's neighbours think and do because one is afraid not to think and do it: "Regardless of whether one is a writer or a reader, one's task consists first of all in mastering a life which is one's own, not imposed or prescribed from without…" Any such prescription will lead to cliché or catastrophe or both – "no matter how noble its appearance may be", Brodsky added (*On Grief and Reason*, p.47).

p.49 *Self-Portrait as a White-Collar Worker (4) – Afterwords*: Pts (1) & (2) of this sequence-within-the-sequence are to be found in *Then and Now – Words in the Dark* and Pt (3) in *From Now to Then*. The 'afterwords' of which Pt (4) consists are therefore an extended postscript to the *Epilogue: Report from Munich – 'The Erlking's Daughter'*, which concludes Pt (3).

As common in painting as it is in literature, the 'self-portrait as...' is, potentially, a more fanciful and also more complex genre than the straight self-portrait; and many artists and writers from Botticelli to Picasso and from Chaucer to James Joyce have exploited its double-edged capacity for criticizing a) the role in question and b) oneself for playing it. Thus Titian paints himself as King Midas in *The Flaying of Marsyas* (1570), and Rembrandt as a drunken Prodigal Son toasting the viewer (1638). In his first preparatory drawing for his famous etching, *The Sleep* (or *Dream*) *of Reason Begets Monsters* (1787), Goya incorporates no less than three portraits of himself – not only as the dreamer but as two disembodied heads among howling gargoyles, bats, dogs, a donkey and a lynx... A peculiarity of all four parts of *Self-Portrait as a White-Collar Worker* is that the poems and translations of which the sequence consists are presented throughout as *by* the persona as well as about him, whose identity is thus built up – in fact, develops – as time goes on (in Pt (4) ca. 4–5 years). Of course, in any *Self-Portrait as...* the artist himself need never have played the role in question in actual life – art is no more than analogous to life, after all. Chaucer may never in fact have been a Canterbury pilgrim – let alone one so incapable of telling an interesting tale in decent verse that the Host has to cut him off (see 'Chaucers Tale of Thopas' in *The Canterbury Tales*). Although Joyce was himself an *Artist* and once *a Young Man*, many of the details of his *(Self-)Portrait* are obviously fictional. "The other one" – the one who contrives his literature – Borges wrote, in the hall of mirrors which is *Borges and I*, "is the one things happen to." But whether or not *I* was once a white-collar worker ("I am quite aware of his perverse custom of falsifying and magnifying things" Borges continued), the background of Pt (4) of the sequence, or the landscape in which it is set, is again Bavaria and the city of Munich – where I confess to really having lived since 1973.

p.51 **the German landscape Primo Levi / Found "rich and civilized"**: At the end of Levi's novel, *If Not Now, When?*, there is a briefly startling moment when its narrator – one of a group of Russian Jewish partisans passing through South Germany in 1945 with the aim of reaching Palestine – observes from their train, after all the German-induced horror and devastation he has witnessed, "the fertile fields, the lakes, the farms and towns of the Upper Palatinate, then of Bavaria. Neither he nor any of his companions had ever inhabited a land so rich and civilized." These observations are the more striking because one knows that Primo Levi himself passed through Bavaria by train on his journey home to Turin from Auschwitz. And the richness and civilization of the German equivalent of the English Lake District – one of the most picturesque *and* sublime landscapes of Europe, surely – remain a mystery when one contemplates what emerged from and in some sense returned to it only a lifetime ago. Rational analysis helps, of course, but something was set loose for which we have no words (in *A Vision* Yeats spoke of "the new era … bringing its stream of irrational force"), killing upwards of fifty million people in six years, and perpetrating in the process atrocities which no mind can imagine. Or even, perhaps, remember – given, that is, the practically universal (and therefore 'banal') human tendency, following "the devices and desires of our own hearts", not only to justify or excuse but to falsify or simply erase what we have left undone and what we have done. *The Book of Common Prayer* continues, "Spare thou them, O God, who confess their faults." But how confess the unspeakable? When the prophet Jeremiah lamented, "Cursed is the man that trusteth in man… For the heart is deceitful above all things, and desperately wicked," he added: "*Who can know it?*" (XIX.9)

p.51 **an outing with the firm / The previous summer:** In Pts (1)–(3) of the sequence, the – obviously English – persona is imagined as having worked for "an electronics communications multinational" first of all in England and then in Munich. His wife (as she herself later mentions) was born in a Bavarian village in the last months of the war.

p.52 **Thirty-three *Sterbebilder*, in a frame:** In South Germany, as in other Catholic parts of the world, a photograph of the deceased – a *Sterbebild* – is sometimes found on gravestones. It is also common practice to include such a picture with the dates of birth and death and a quotation or short text in a leaflet to be distributed to friends and relatives or displayed in the church itself as a memento. Of the sorts of men from Hemhof (Chiemgau) who died in the war, the boys and those without uniform may well have been called up into the *Volkssturm* in the last few months of it – a last-ditch Dad's Army, as it has been called, given minimum training, black arm bands and a rifle before being sent to defend the Reich… One might expect more than **A Nazi or two**. However, fascist movements had trouble almost everywhere in appealing to the genuinely traditional elements in rural society (Hobsbawm, *Age of Extremes*, ch.4). Not for nothing does Oskar Mazarath in Günter Grass's *The Tin Drum* begin his tale of inner resistance to oppression with his Kashubian grandmother hiding his grandfather from the police under her voluminous skirts in the middle of a rainy potato field – and conceiving Oskar's mother at one and the same time! Furthermore, although the Catholic church, which has flourished in South Germany since the first millenium, dithered between supporting and opposing Hitler's regime – they had the same enemies but not the same goals – it was never fascist… For all his initial policy of attempting to co-opt the churches,

Hitler's ideology was, of course, profoundly un- and anti-Christian. So much so that his incompetent 'philosopher', Alfred Rosenberg's thirty articles of the 'National Reich Church' read like a mere travesty of established religion. For example:

> 5. The National Church is determined to exterminate irrevocably ... the strange and foreign Christian faiths imported into Germany in the ill-omened year 800.
> 13. The National Church demands the immediate cessation of the publishing and dissemination of the Bible in Germany...
> 15. The National Church declares that to it, and therefore to the German nation, it has been decided that the Führer's *Mein Kampf* is the greatest of all documents. It ... not only contains the greatest but it embodies the purest and truest ethics for the present and future life of our nation.
> 19. On the altars there must be nothing but *Mein Kampf* (to the German nation and therefore to God the most sacred book) and to the left of the altar a sword.

And so on. Possibly even to Hitler's relief, the National Reich Church never got past the planning stage – although the articles themselves were published in *The New York Times* as early as January, 1942.

p.53 **Stammtisch**: In a society in which much value is placed on togetherness and belonging, who sits where and with whom are matters of some importance. Thus every Bavarian *Wirtshaus* has a table – the *Stammtisch* – where only regulars and their guests are allowed to sit or where others may only sit with the landlord or *Wirt*'s permission. Other meanings of *Stamm* are: tribe, stock or lineage, permanent team or workforce, tree-trunk.

p.54 **He'd volunteered / Before being press-ganged by the *Waffen-SS*, etc.**: As *Reichsführer-SS*, Himmler was constantly trying to expand the mandate and thus the size of the SS. In the occupied territories, particularly in the East, there was no great problem in finding ethnic Germans (and others) who were willing to sign up. However, in the Reich itself many young men were anti-*Waffen-SS* and SS-recruiters were sometimes reduced to scouring the Hitler Youth and obligatory *Arbeitsdienst* (Labour Service) where they virtually press-ganged 'volunteers'. One way of escaping the clutches of the SS was to volunteer first for service in the *Wehrmacht*, whose reputation was less unsavoury, before one was called up. Whether there was in fact much danger of being conscripted into the *Waffen-SS* against one's will in so remote a village as Stephanskirchen is hard to tell. However, the historian Joachim Fest admitted to having joined the *Wehrmacht* for this reason as a young man. His father Johannes was a Catholic school-teacher who lost his position because he refused to join the Party: "Everybody else may join," he said, "*aber ich nicht*" – "but not me" – when his wife pleaded with him to say the right thing for the sake of the family. Johannes also took the view that "one does not volunteer for Hitler's criminal war", although he later told his son: "You weren't wrong – but I was the one who was right." His view was perhaps righter than either of them knew at the time. Fest himself was taken prisoner in France, where the war was conducted, for the most part, with comparative restraint and in accordance with international law. Elsewhere, especially in eastern Europe and the Balkans, this was not the case and, though some notorious atrocities (for example, towards the end of the war in Italy) were 'explained' as military tactics, the post-war myth of the relative decency of the *Wehrmacht* has been gradually dispelled by later historians.

p.55 **The Jews were *different*, etc.**: The series of rather commonplace explanations in this section of the poem offered by the old man, as reported and elaborated on by his interlocutor, for the unprecedented flood of anti-Semitism which culminated in the massacres and calculated genocide of the Second World War have the usual effect, it will be noticed, of softening or reducing the things which really happened. If this is sometimes the result of prevarication and/or ignorance, it was also in fact the case that so much of what happened was indescribable:

> Mere anarchy is loosed upon the world,
> The blood-dimmed tide is loosed, and everywhere
> The ceremony of innocence is drowned…
> (W.B.Yeats, *The Second Coming*)

What really happened – "A gaze blank and pitiless as the sun" – could scarcely be grasped or clearly retained by anyone's memory:

> The darkness drops again; but now I know
> That twenty centuries of stony sleep
> Were vexed to nightmare by a rocking cradle,
> And what rough beast, its hour come round at last,
> Slouches towards Bethlehem to be born?

Hence the very great importance, as is everywhere recognized, of books of witness such as Elie Wiesel's *Night* or – written within a few months of the event – Primo Levi's *If This is a Man*, whose literary strategies have been described (by Anthony Rudolf in *At an Uncertain Hour*) as enabling, paradoxically, "the saying of the unsayable, the bearing witness to the unbearable". Levi himself was (of course) aware of the dangers of his "war on behalf of memory" (Rudolf): "Perhaps one cannot, what is more one must not, understand what happened," he wrote in his 'Afterword' to *If This Is a Man* and *The Truce*, "because to understand is almost to justify." Similarly, to explain is almost to excuse. ***Macht mit***, for example, is the virtual equivalent of "Come and join us" or "All for one and one for all!" And **"The socialism of idiots"** was used by the German working-class socialist leader, August Bebel, to dismiss the rise of political anti-Semitism in the late nineteenth century… In *Stephanskirchen (1)*, the persona's relative ignorance of the terrible excesses and sheer scale of man's inhumanity in the Second World War is not untypical of his generation – as he acknowledges later. The more aware that one becomes of what happened, though, the less sense it makes. The virulence of Hitler's own blind and fanatical anti-Semitism was presumably psychopathic in origin. The superficially 'political' uses to which he and other top Nazis deliberately put their openly racist ideology, on the other hand, and the reactions to it of ordinary sane individuals all over Europe are in some ways more disturbing. Levi epitomizes Auschwitz in a famous few lines: "Driven by thirst, I eyed a fine icicle outside the window, within arm's reach. I opened the window and broke off the icicle but at once a large, heavy guard prowling outside brutally snatched it away from me. '*Warum?*' I asked him in my poor German. '*Hier ist kein warum*' (there is no why here) he replied, pushing me back inside…" And yet if Auschwitz, by common consent, was humanity's nadir, the inexplicable happened everywhere. How *could* anyone 'explain' the spontaneous orgy of anti-Semitic violence and looting which erupted in Vienna, of all places, on the eve of the *Anschluß*, before the German army had as much as arrived, when the Jewish community was so terrified and disoriented that an estimated five hundred people committed suicide? Or even the merciless enthusiasm – taking the SS itself by surprise – with which the local inhabitants of less sophisticated areas in the Ukraine and the Baltic states, for example, participated in public massacres in the market-places of villages and towns, or in municipal gardens and recreation spots, until Himmler's deputy, Reinhard Heydrich, sensing an opportunity, ordered his men to encourage townsfolk and peasantry to begin "attempts at self-cleansing on the part of anti-communist or anti-Semitic elements", permitting a further spate of atrocities?

Elsewhere, it was the political élite which was ready to take advantage of Hitler's lethal brew of intense nationalism and equally intense racism. For example, in Romania – Germany's ally from 1940/41 onward – where much of the country's administration, under the leadership of General Ion Antonescu (or the *Conducator*, as he was known), was already anti-Semitic: "Romanian anti-Semitism had been a matter of international concern as far back as the nineteenth century; now, under the aegis of National Socialist Germany, the country's rulers saw the chance for radical measures of the kind the democracies had always prevented them from undertaking" (M. Mazower, *Hitler's Empire*, 2008). In all such countries and communities, in other words, Nazi racist ideology and propaganda, plus the harsh and ruthless example of the SS and the *Wehrmacht*, not only permitted but actively encouraged the local populace to act on its worst impulses – impulses which had formerly been held in control by cultural, legal and/or political restraints. The result, in Romania as elsewhere, was previously unimaginable violence directed against civilians, and especially the Jews. On the 28/29 June 1941 alone between 13,000 and 15,000 people died in the enforced 'evacuation' of the border town of Jassy. The doors of Christian houses in the town were marked with a cross to distinguish them, and soldiers, gendarmes, policemen, and hundreds of civilians rampaged through the streets, broke into houses and brought their occupants back under arrest to police headquarters, where more than 1,000 were gunned down in the grounds when the Germans opened fire at random. Many Jews were killed or attacked wherever they were found. Thousands of others died of dehydration in the overcrowded trains transporting them out of Romania in the summer heat. By mid-1942 only 14,000 of the 275,000 Jews of Bessarabia and Bukhovina remained in the region: the rest had either died or been driven over the old border of the country into German-occupied Ukraine. When Romanian and German troops finally took Odessa (in October 1941), a delayed-action Soviet mine blew up the Romanian commander and sixty soldiers. By this time, the identification of the Jews with Bolshevism and with partisans and saboteurs in general was virtually routine (although it had almost no basis in fact) and thousands were immediately hanged or shot throughout the night in a spontaneous 'punishment action'. The next day, Antonescu – one of the *Führer*'s favourite strongmen – ordered that a further 18,000 'Communists' should be killed: i.e. reprisals of about 300 to one. In fact, an estimated 25–30,000 Jews were rounded up with the help of Ukrainian auxiliaries and shot or burned alive in warehouses at Dalnic, ten miles west of the city. By the end of the occupation, more than 300,000 Romanian and Ukrainian Jews are estimated to have perished.

In the end, the only 'explanation' for such appallingly inhuman – and all *too* human – behaviour which is not also an excuse for it (and these, of course, are only a few of countless possible examples from the Second World War, not to mention what came after it in Stalinist Russia, Communist China, Cambodia, Rwanda, Iraq, and elsewhere) may be that offered by Joseph Brodsky in his magisterial yet disarming open letter to the President of Czechoslovakia, Vaclav Havel, *Letter to a President* (1993), in which he frankly mocks "the premise, however qualified, of man's goodness, of his notion of himself as either a fallen or a possible angel". Having lived the first thirty-two years of his life under Russian Communist totalitarianism – which he saw less as a political problem than "a breakdown of humanity, a human problem, a problem of our species" – Brodsky tended to the view instead that much of the twentieth century might serve as a reminder of Original Sin: "not such a heady concept", he explains – "translated into common parlance, it means that man is dangerous…" Brodsky saw the commonest source of this danger in what one might call "unenlightened self-interest", and comments that, at the very least, "it seems more prudent to build society on the premise that man is evil than the premise of his goodness… Maybe the real civility, Mr President, is not to create illusions."

The reason why this explanation is not an excuse is that, although always a danger to himself and his fellow creatures, man is also and at all times, no matter what the conditions, endowed with free will. As Brodsky's letter implies throughout, each one of us can always *choose* – between barbarism and mutual tolerance, between the rule of the strongest or the most ruthlessly ambitious and 'live and let live'. Johannes Fest could not have put this more clearly: "Everybody else may join – *aber ich nicht*." The human ability to categorize, to decide on *which* devices and desires we mean to follow, to sort reality into mental boxes such as 'us' and 'them', if it helps to preserve our sanity, is capable as well of permitting us to view as 'normal' acts of individual cruelty, mass-murder or mass-destruction. The springs of pity, it plainly seems, can be turned off at will – individually or, more often, collectively. In other words, "I *think*, therefore I *act*" (cp. 'The Dance of Death', *Boccaccio in Florence*, p.28). As Hitler and Goebbels clearly understood: hence the enormous pains they took not only with what Hitler in *Mein Kampf* called "spiritual and physical terror" but with propaganda, rhetoric and stage-management, each of which is a form of art – debased and perverted in this case but practised nevertheless by men who regarded themselves as, among other things, artists and connoisseurs whose duty and mission it was to defend German "richness and civilization" against the machinations of international Jewry and the hordes of Asia. Individual and collective feelings of every sort – from pity to heartlessness or sadism, from euphoria to loathing, from ecstasy to real or apparent madness – occur or run to excess within certain frameworks. The more we allow these frameworks, or our 'devices', to be manipulated and perverted, the more manipulable and perverse will be our desires. The demonstrable fact, in other words, that human thinking permits or forbids – facilitates or hinders – clarifies or confuses human action matters immensely: "The world is *led* by mind."

p.55 **Mercy or pity was mere Christian weakness:** Orders and directives such as that of Hans Frank, the Nazi governor of much of Poland, to his staff in preparation for the Final Solution – "Gentlemen, I must ask you to rid yourselves of all feelings of pity" – became commonplace during the Third Reich, many of them deriving directly or ultimately from Hitler himself. As a connoisseur of German culture, Borges was at first as distressed and puzzled by this as anyone. However, his excellent story, *Deutsches Requiem*, is a powerful study of how a highly educated and civilized concentration camp commandant, Otto Dietrich zur Linde, became convinced that "Essentially, Nazism is an act of morality, a purging of corrupted humanity... The world was dying of Judaism and from that sickness of Judaism, the faith of Jesus: we taught it violence and the faith of the sword." Thus not only **Perverts and numbskulls** strove to exterminate the Jews but cultivated intellectuals such as Borges' hero (he sees himself as heroic) and anyone else to whom, for whatever reason, the Nazis' ideology and propaganda appealed. These ranged from young Romantic adventurers (***So why not go**, he'd thought, **and** make *things change!*) such as Odilo Globocnik in Poland, who became the driving power behind Operation Reinhard, which killed 1,200,000 Polish Jews in 1941–42 alone, to cold-blooded SS bureaucrats such as Eichmann – proud to the last of his organizational efficiency – or the highly intelligent Werner Best, who was one of the first to contemplate racial extermination openly. Ambitious men such as these relished the career opportunity which the administrative challenges of the *Judenfrage* (Jewish question) offered them, and were out to impress their bosses (above all, Himmler). Beneath them, there was the whole bureaucracy of *Ja*-sayers who, as Raul Hilberg showed in *The Destruction of the European Jews*, were knowingly involved in the genocide. Hilberg's pages on 'The Perpetrators' (ch.7) include a convincing account of how ordinary white-collar workers persuaded themselves that what they were doing was at least not bad – or not *as* bad as what others were doing – and in any case no more than part of a large-scale, justifiable and *necessary* operation... Even those who did the killing were to draw a sharp line "between killings pursuant to orders and killings induced by desire. In the former case a man was thought to have overcome the 'weaknesses' of 'Christian morality'; in the latter case he was overcome by his own baseness".

p.56 *'Pleasure generates submission'*: This begins a series of quotations from *Then and Now – Words in the Dark* ('Paradise Island', 'Heine's Grave', 'The Park on Sunday') and *From Now to Then* ('Lazarus') – on themes relating to this section of the poem.

p.57 **How nations vie like firms – how firms deploy / Their workforce like a peace-time army**: Hitler himself had little knowledge of or interest in economics, and tended to prioritize short-term policies which amounted, especially in the East, to not much more than plundering occupied territories. Otherwise, the ease with which the belligerent mentality can mesh with the business mentality and the latter feed into the former so as to cooperate in an actual war-effort was everywhere apparent during the Third Reich. "The point about really big business", Eric Hobsbawm drily observed, "is that it can come to terms with any regime that does not actually expropriate it, and that any regime must come to terms with it." Nevertheless, the Nazis' elimination of the Communist Party in 1933 and their promise to do the same with elections and free trade unions and to defy Versailles and the League of Nations by re-arming was all profoundly attractive to the likes of Krupp, United Steel and IG Farben. At a meeting in February 1933 hosted by Dr Schach, Hitler's chief financial expert, Hitler and Göring announced their intentions. Krupp and others were enthusiastic in expressing their "gratitude for having given us so clear a picture". Dr Schach then passed the hat on behalf of the Party: "I collected three million marks," he recalled at Nuremberg…

With free trade unions out of the way, management felt much freer in dealing with its workforce: "Indeed, the fascist 'leadership principle' [*Führerprinzip*] was what most bosses and business executives applied to their subordinates in their own businesses, and fascism gave it authoritative justification" (Hobsbawm). If peace seemed initially preferable, once war had broken out, firms like IG Farben took full advantage of it: "Following close behind the troops, they dismissed Jewish employees and accepted Nazis on company boards in return for being allowed to take over non-German businesses" (Mazower).

In western Europe many businesses prospered during the war, as businessmen saw little point in not cooperating with the Germans. However, in the East the Germans and above all Göring's enormous Reichswerke HG took over everything they possibly could. By mid-1944 the Reichswerke HG, with over 400,000 employees from Austria to Russia, working in coal, mineral extraction, chemicals, armaments, iron and steel and other metals, and manufacturing in general, was probably the largest industrial conglomerate in the world. Göring attempted to take over western European industries as well, but experienced businessmen, bankers and very large firms such as Unilever and Philips saw the war as an opportunity to build on their long-established relationships, and he was less successful. Moreover, the *Wehrmacht* and even Hitler took the pragmatic view that as long as Belgian, Dutch and Danish industry continued to produce what the Germans wanted (in Holland alone about 20,000 firms "offered no resistance to the acceptance of German contracts"), there was no need to interfere. After about 1940, increasing chaos and partial or piecemeal solutions in the absence of any long-term economic policy somewhat weakened Göring's position. But it is clear that the *Reichsmarschall* and former Luftwaffe ace would in peacetime have made an ace businessman.

p.57 *"History is to blame"*: In Joyce's *Ulysses*, the condescending English student of the Irish, Haines, explains to Stephen Dedalus and Buck Mulligan, "We feel in England that we have treated you rather unfairly. It seems that history is to blame." This is, of course, one of the commonest of excuses in the guise of an explanation: "God, isn't he dreadful? [Mulligan] said frankly. A ponderous Saxon. He thinks you're not a gentleman. God, these bloody English. Bursting with money and indigestion. Because he comes from Oxford." Mulligan's "British Beatitudes" are well known: "Beer, beef, business, bibles, bulldogs, battleships, buggery and bishops." By adapting *The Odyssey* in the ways it does and at the time it did (1914–21), *Ulysses* implicitly and explicitly shows that there are other, more enlightened forms of 'heroism' than the military. In the Nighttown episode, Stephen addresses the Hue and Cry pursuing himself and Bloom:

> STEPHEN: (*With elaborate gestures, breathing deeply and slowly*) You are my guests. The uninvited. By virtue of the fifth of George and seventh of Edward. History to blame....
> PRIVATE COMPTON: He doesn't half want a thick ear, the blighter. Biff him, Harry.
> LORD TENNYSON: (*In Union Jack blazer and cricket flannels, bareheaded, flowingbearded*) Theirs not to reason why...
> PRIVATE CARR: (*To Stephen*) What's that you're saying about my king?...
> EDWARD THE SEVENTH: (*Slowly, solemnly but indistinctly*) Peace, perfect peace...
> PRIVATE CARR: (*To Stephen*) Say it again.
> STEPHEN: (*Nervous, friendly, pulls himself up*) I understand your point

of view, though I have no king myself for the moment… A discussion is difficult down here. But this is the point. You die for your country, suppose. (*He places his arm on Private Carr's sleeve*) Not that I wish it for you. But I say: let my country die for me. Up to the present it has done so. I don't want it to die. Damn death. Long live life!
EDWARD THE SEVENTH: (*Levitates over heaps of slain in the garb and with the halo of Joking Jesus, a white jujube in his phosphorescent face*)

    My methods are new and are causing surprise:

    To make the blind see I throw dust in their eyes…

BLOOM: (*To Stephen*) Come home. You'll get into trouble.
STEPHEN: (*Swaying*) I don't avoid it. He provokes my intelligence…
PRIVATE CARR: Here. What are you saying about my king?
STEPHEN: (*Throws up his hands*) O, this is too monotonous! Nothing. He wants my money and my life for some brutish empire of his. Money I haven't. (*He searches his pockets vaguely*) Gave it to someone.

p.60 **They wanted peace, not war, to have the last word**: The illusion that war can lead to any sort of lasting peace is at least as old as the 'Heroique Stanza' – thus named by Dryden in the title of his poem on the death of Oliver Cromwell – which *Stephanskirchen (1)* and *(2)* adapt to their own purposes: "Our former Cheifs", says Dryden, were all war-mongers –

> Warre, our consumption, was their gainful trade,
> We inward bled while they prolong'd our pain:
> He fought to end our fighting, and assaid
> To stanch the blood by breathing of the vein.

In Shakespeare this futile self-deception dominates the words and deeds of assorted rulers, from Henry IV – the guilt-ridden initiator of approximately one hundred years of civil war – to the ruthless politico, Henry VII, who aspired to end them:

> In God's name, cheerly on, courageous friends,
> To reap the harvest of perpetual peace
> By this one bloody trial of sharp war.
>   *Richard III*, V.ii

p.60 **And yet Ernst Jandl, etc.**: Ernst Jandl (1925–2000) was a leading

Viennese avant-garde poet and dramatist. The extraordinary story of his wartime experiences has recently been clarified by the publication of *Briefe aus dem Krieg* (Letters from the War, 2005), which illustrates how difficult – but not impossible – it was for young men in the wrong place at the wrong time to avoid fighting for Hitler. Although not primarily thought of as a war poet, Jandl's conscription into the German army in 1943, after finishing school, left its mark on his poetry and also his life. Cp. *after jandl*.

p.61 **Or what he'd done and not done – must have seen...:** Many examples of what the old man might have seen as a young soldier in the East have already been mentioned in these notes: the effects of political and historical anti-Semitism in Vienna, the Balkan states, Poland (by the end of 1942 public unease in Germany itself about the – secret – Final Solution was being fed by soldiers returning from the East), and Romania and the Ukraine. Even one of the most notorious Ukrainian atrocities, at Babi Yar – a ravine near Kiev, where over 33,000 Jews were machine-gunned in a matter of days by the German SS and Ukrainian guards – was in fact a 'punishment action' demanded by the *Wehrmacht* after delayed Soviet mines blew up some of the newly installed military administration of the city... Hilberg, in his classic work, lists numerous shootings and other war-crimes in eastern Europe which the *Wehrmacht* either demanded or was involved in, or at which soldiers were present as voyeurs (some of them taking photographs) – a practice which some officers attempted to prevent. As for the Russian campaign itself, its horrors will never be fully documented. The conditions in which Soviet prisoners of war had to be kept, for example, confounded even old and experienced soldiers: "So unbelievably many have starved to death", wrote one sixty-five-year-old former Wilhelmine officer in his diary in March 1942 of the 30,000 POWs he and his 200 men had to guard with neither sufficient provisions nor medical supplies nor proper accommodation: "Of millions of prisoners only a few thousands are capable of working... Many are ill with typhus and the rest are so weak and pitiful that they can't work in this state." As conditions behind the front continued to deteriorate, cases of cannibalism were dealt with by shooting the offenders ("The men there are beasts" was Hitler's comment – "a bestial degeneration of humanity [*Menscheitsentartung*]"...) Altogether, it took only a few months, in the winter of 1941–42 for the master race to allow more than two million Soviet POWs to perish in such crowded holding pens, out of sight and largely unrecorded. More than a million more died by the end of the war – most of them under *Wehrmacht* supervision. Small wonder that German generals themselves believed, as recent research has discovered, that "the *Führer* wishes for the decimation of the Slavic masses". Of course, such research might in general be less necessary, were it not for "the universal (and therefore 'banal') human tendency" noted above, to normalize what happened – as even slips of the tongue such as **"I was a long way east / Of here by then. And didn't see a thing…"** (p.52) unconsciously illustrate.

p.67 **surfacetranslation (1)**: Jandl's own *oberflächenübersetzung*, on which this poem is based, is of Wordsworth's "My heart leaps up when I behold / A rainbow in the sky": *mai hart lieb zapfen eibe hold / er renn bohr in sees kai*, etc. The idea is varied somewhat in **surfacetranslation (2)** by using a (shortened) poem of Jandl's own as the 'original' and also by preserving its word-play – on *Philosophie* – albeit with a different emphasis: *viel* means 'many' and *vieh* means 'cattle' or 'pigs' in the sense of disgusting people.

p.70 **otto's mops**: The German word *Mops* means pug-dog. In Jandl's poem, however, Otto *addresses* his dog as Mops – here taken to be his name for it.

p.77 **light and reft**: One of the 'thiggest contusions' of right and left was faked into the very name of the Nazi Party. After the Party had come to power in 1933 and the independent Left – the Communists and free trade unions – had been destroyed, there was much clamour for a 'second revolution', i.e. for a radical National *Socialism*, which would destroy the Right as well. The phrase "the second revolution" had been coined by Ernst Röhm, the Chief of Staff of the ca. two-million-strong SA. But Hitler's guiding political principle of exploiting rather than directly opposing powerful institutions – business, the Army, the President – led him, in June 1934, to purge the SA and remove Röhm entirely: see *Death and Brandner Caspar*. For Hitler, Nazi socialist slogans had become no more than a means of keeping the masses (including six million unemployed) on his side on his way to power. And he in fact continued to woo the workers in one way and another… As for Jandl, he seems never to have been taken in by the Party's weasel words. While still at school, he had successfully avoided Hitler Youth meetings and become adept at keeping his head down. Even after conscription he managed – by taking every military training course available, pleading nervous disorders, and going AWOL (twice) – to get out of active service. Needless to say, some parts of this strategy were extremely dangerous but, wiser than his eighteen years, Jandl took every advantage he could of the growing disorder of the last two years of the war. Eventually, in November 1944, he was sent to the western front. This was, relatively speaking, a piece of luck since his plan was to defect if he possibly could, and on the eastern front no one defected to the Russians. As it was, he saw three months of front-line action before he managed to cross the line to the Americans without getting shot. Jandl later explained to his editor, Klaus Siblewski, that he had felt buoyed up through these adventures by his sense of himself as someone with poetry to write, on the one hand, and by his family on the other, to whom the *Letters* referred to above were addressed in such a way as to relieve them of worry, as far as was possible... After being sent by the Americans to POW camp at Stockbridge in England, he found himself more or less out of danger. He became camp interpreter and improved his English, which he then studied on returning to Vienna in 1946, where he worked as a grammar-school teacher until his writings permitted him to retire.

p.79 **i have nothing / to make a poem**: Ernst Jandl's writing is in many respects an act of existential anti-heroism, as this formulation of its contents indicates. Although he defected with flying colours, the war continued to affect both his physical and mental health. He described himself, with typical black humour, as a pessimist with a sense of black humour. By way of comment on his un- and even anti-poetic poetry, he explained that the war didn't sing. The section '*krieg und so*' ('war and all that') in his celebrated book, *Laut und Luise* (1966), gives some small hint of the horror and sheer word-destroying mechanical racket of the front. Elsewhere he wrote: "... he always had something to say, and he always knew one could say it in this way or in that way; and so he was never concerned with what he was saying but with how he said it, since there is no alternative to what one has to say but an unlimited number of possible ways of saying it. there are poets who say all sorts of things, and always in the same way. to write like this never interested him; because in the end there is only one thing to be said, but over and over again, always in new ways."

Without wishing to detract from Ernst Jandl's lifelong opposition of brilliant formal invention and pitch-black humour to the nothingness of everything, including the chaos of mechanized war, one can enter a plea as well for singing – not, perhaps, *of* but *over against* it. If things in themselves have (as *contents* implies) no inherent meaning but if human consciousness nevertheless gives them, with the help of one's ability to perceive, experience, think and express oneself, what meanings they appear to have, then when reality itself doesn't sing, can not the poet? Or can not anyone? And over against anything? After all, what W.B. Yeats wrote of old men in *Byzantium* is true, if less obviously true, of men and women of any age:

> An aged man is but a paltry thing,
> A tattered coat upon a stick, unless
> Soul clap its hands and sing, and louder sing

For every tatter in its mortal dress.

p.79 ***Death and Dr Hornbrook***: In Robert Burns's humorously ironic, tough-minded poem (which includes a self-portrait as a not-so-innocent by-stander), Death complains to the poet of being cheated of his victims, on the one hand, by the quack Dr Hornbrook's infallible medicines – against which his dart and scythe are helpless – and, on the other, by his activities as a poisoner:

> This night I'm free to take my aith
> > That Hornbrook's skill
> Has clad a score in their last claith,
> > By drap an' pill.

For example, bearing in mind Burns's wife's wry comment, "Oor Rab should hae had twa wives":

> A bonnie lass, ye kenned her name,
> Some ill-brewn drink had hoved her wame;
> She trusts hersel', to hide the shame,
> > In Hornbrook's care;
> Horn sent her off to her lang hame,
> > To hide it there.

Etc.

p.79 **Franz, Ritter von Kobell**: Franz von Kobell (1803–1882) became a professor of mineralogy in Munich in 1826 but is nowadays mainly remembered for his verses and tales in Bavarian dialect. ***Die Gschicht von Brandner-Kasper*** is a ***Schwank*** or humorous narrative of the legendary practical-joker variety. A *Schwank* is also an unlikely or tall tale of any kind, or a theatrical farce.

p.81 **At nearby Gindlalm**: Gindlalm was and still is a *Wirtshaus* for hikers and locals as well as a working Alpine farm at the top of the path from Schliersee to Tegernsee. If one turns left after Gindlalm there is a path across and down to the other end of the Schliersee through a village called Neuhaus. As the war drew to a close with the unstoppable advance of the Red Army, Hans Frank, who, as the Nazi governor of much of Poland, had played host, as it were, to four of the six main killing centres of the Final Solution – not to mention his part in the wholesale slaughter of Polish civilians in the General Government (Poland itself and Polish culture were to disappear) – made an undignified run for it and ended up, with his family and closest entourage, at his villa in Neuhaus, which is nowadays a quiet resort. One has the impression that many top Nazis were adept at evading the reality of the war around them. In the former residence of the Polish kings at Wawel and in a private castle of his own near Kraków, whose Jewish population fell from 68,000 to 500, Frank had held court from 1941–45 with pomp and extravagance, surrounded by his family and numerous hangers-on, patronizing artists of all kinds, hosting concerts, and attending the opera. As one witness at Nuremberg said, Frank's court was "an oasis where no one noticed the war", and "even short-hand typists led a life such as one reads about in the Arabian Nights". Frank's fur-draped wife, Brigitte – herself a short-hand typist and her husband's former secretary – considered herself the 'Queen of Poland' and when the Americans arrived in Neuhaus to find the Franks holding court again among masterpieces by Leonardo, Rembrandt, Rubens, Dürer and others, which they had confiscated "for safe-keeping", she welcomed the end of hostilities and looked forward to a "normal life", confident she had done no wrong. At his trial in Nuremberg, her self-pitying, deluded and theatrical husband admitted some of his crimes – as witnessed by W.L. Shirer, who in *The Rise and Fall of the Third Reich* (1960) described him as "having become in the end contrite and, as he said, having rediscovered God, whose forgiveness he begged". Nevertheless, the Americans hanged him. The Café-Pension Bergfrieden, where the General Government had its last headquarters, is now a wellness centre.

p.84 **As drunk / as Tam o'Shanter**: Robert Burns's highly inventive, humorous and intelligent narrative poem, one of the finest of its age, became increasingly popular – together with his love songs and other poems (though not, officially, his bawdy *Merry Muses of Caledonia*) – throughout the nineteenth century for reasons which have as much to do with the nature of Romanticism (its exaggerated interest in the 'primitive', in the supernatural, in almost any form of anti-rationalism) as with the actual qualities of Burns's writing. In fact, a hard-headed sense of reality distinguished Burns (as it did Goya and, later, Heine) from most of his contemporaries. From this point of view, one can read *Tam o'Shanter* as implicitly posing the question shortly to be asked by Brandner Caspar's grandson, **What really happened?** (p.86). All anyone *knew*, after all, was that Tam got drunk and came home late through very bad weather on Maggie, who lost her tail. As with Brandner Caspar's version of events, and those of Balthazar and Melchior later, the questions remain of who said who did what and why.

p.84 *To My Bed*: Much of this poem-within-the-poem has been borrowed from Burns's *Verses to My Bed*. Surprisingly, considering its subject – a stroke of Burnsian genius – *Verses to My Bed* is in English and not in his native lowland Scots. As usual, this cramps his style – which is perhaps some slight excuse for the changes here made as if by the persona on behalf of Brandner Caspar, a character who would have been much to Burns's taste.

p.88 *"What is truth?"* Amid the tangle of lies, deceptions and self-deceptions which we generally regard, or pretend to regard, as everyday communication – and then as history – certain individuals have always been remarkable for their refusal to play the game. According to St John, when Jesus was questioned in the Roman judgement hall by Pontius Pilatus as to whether he was the king of the Jews, Jesus explained to him: "My kingdom is not of this world: if my kingdom were of this world, then would my servants fight… To this end was I born, and for this cause came I into the world, that I should bear witness unto the truth. Every one that is of the truth heareth my voice." It was in reply to this that Pilate asked him, "What is truth?" (*John XVIII*. 36–38)… When Stephen Dedalus is questioned by Cranly towards the end of *A Portrait of the Artist as a Young Man* as to whether he felt sure that Jesus was not the Son of God, Stephen answers, "I am not at all sure of it… He is more like a son of God than a son of Mary." As for Pilate, he behaved like a son of Rome and, handing Jesus over to his accusers, washed his hands of him.

p.90 **What with the death as well, in the war, / Of Georg, his firstborn:** If there had in fact been a Brandner family tomb at Gmund (cp. p.86), on the opposite side of the Tegernsee to Wiessee, its later inscriptions at that time might have informed the reader of the following dates of birth and death:

Traudl Brandner	1740 – 1794
Georg	1768 – 1800
Brandner Caspar	1724 – 1804 (*missing presumed dead*)
Balthazar	1745 – 1828
Toni	1770 – 1830
Melchior	1750 – 1840

If Toni returned from the war in 1805, Brandner Caspar's grandson was presumably born between then and about 1810. According to the *Postscript* (p.93), he died without issue in 1870, leaving von Kobell free to publish his own version of whatever happened.

p.96 *Case Studies, 1941–1945*: As its title implies, this section of the

Self-Portrait as... keeps as close as may be to historical reality as represented by its main sources. In addition to the writings of Hilberg, Levi, Mazower, Shirer and others already mentioned, these include: Curzio Malaparte, *Kaputt* (no. (vii)); *Das Daimler-Benz Buch*, ed. A. Ebbinghaus, 1987 (no.s (xiii) and (xiv)); *Konzentrationslager Dokument F321*, ed. P. Neitzke and M. Weinmann, 1988 (no. (xviii)); and, above all, Claude Lanzmann's *Shoah* (no.s (ix), (x), (xii), (xv) and (xvi)). Moreover, the section as a whole owes a particular debt to W. G. Sebald for its passages in prose or what one might think of as the 'case histories' which follow each poem. If *after jandl* can be read as the white-collar worker's acknowledgement of the significance of his wife's remarks towards the end of *Stephanskirchen (1)*, i.e. as a portrayal of his own of another man's efforts to face the truth; and if *Death and Brandner Caspar* represents a consideration of how "thugs or rogues or fools" and others seem capable in general of explaining or justifying their crimes or other misdeeds both to themselves and those around them; *Case Studies* goes on to recreate or re-observe a series of real people in a direct attempt at last to break down, or rather out of, the state of denial regarding the works and words of the Second World War in which many or even most of us still find ourselves, as Sebald patiently and tirelessly demonstrates. Like Sebald as well, the section concentrates for the most part (though not only) on the 'Final Solution of the Jewish Question', as Hitler himself appears to have called it.

p.119 ***diavoli neri***: Dante's most extended treatment of devils is to be found in *Inferno*, Cantos XXI–XXII, where – perhaps by chance (if there is such a thing as chance in such matters) – the Hell of his poem resembles Müller's verbal and Lanzmann's visual descriptions of Auschwitz in a number of ways. More specifically, the mocking devils of Canto XXI are quoted by Primo Levi in ch. 2 of *If This is a Man* as an obliquely ironic comment on the guard who epitomized Auschwitz in the words "*Hier ist kein warum*". As one might expect of an Italian author, there are many other allusions, direct and indirect, to Dante in Levi's writings. The great difference, of course, is that Dante took the view that the inmates of his Hell were tormented *justly*: that is, in Dante's mind at least, there was every reason "why" they should suffer.

p.129 **In twelve mad minutes twelve years of power imploded**: Himmler died, in spite of frantic efforts to pump his stomach, twelve minutes after biting on his cyanide capsule, on 23 May 1945, the gutter having come to power, in Alan Bullock's memorable words (*Hitler, A Study in Tyranny*, p. 270) twelve years earlier, in 1933.

p.130 *They sowed the wind, etc.*: Cp. *Hosea VII.7*: "For they have sown the wind, and they shall reap the whirlwind." Harris's statement of his mission as Commander-in-Chief of Bomber Command – a position to which he was appointed in February 1942 – elevates himself, by implication, to the position not only of God's prophet, or approximate equivalent, but of His agent. This "rather childish delusion" is not helped by the insensitivity of the Biblical reference: Hosea was threatening the Jews themselves with destruction for their impiety in a blast of indignant righteousness resounding with such verses as "Israel hath cast off the thing that is good: the enemy shall pursue him", or "Israel is swallowed up: now shall they be among the Gentiles as a vessel wherein is no pleasure"… As luck would have it, the church at Stephanskirchen was empty when it was bombed, presumably by accident. A partly happy accident, then – whose absurdity, however, is entirely characteristic of the indiscriminate and more often murderous inaccuracy of any such war-time "whirlwind". Harris's strident self-assertiveness and fascination with destruction in general put one in mind of an ill-treated schoolboy with more talented brothers. In 1908, when he was sixteen, his father (who was in the Indian Civil Service) gave him the choice of army or colonies. He went to Rhodesia (Zimbabwe), where he flourished. Later he leap-frogged the army by joining the Royal Flying Corps and serving with distinction in the First World War. Back in the colonies, he cultivated an interest in bombing, first in India, then in Mesopotamia (Iraq, Syria) and Persia (Iran). In Mesopotamia, he was involved in developing the same sort of delayed-action bombs which were dropped together with high-explosive and incendiary bombs in the Second World War with the intention of blowing up rescuers and fire-fighters. While putting down Mesopotamian insurrections against the British with the help of such new devices, Harris famously remarked, "The only thing the Arab understands is the heavy hand." The lessons of his English schooldays were clearly not lost on him and, as a senior officer in Palestine in 1936, he recommended "one 250 lb or 500 lb bomb in each village that speaks out of turn". By the early 1940s these had become 4,000 lb and 8,000 lb bombs in their hundreds and the villages heavily populated German cities.

p.132 **"Just give them sufficient money // To keep them happy, Lord…"**: This outburst of apparent cynicism (cp., however, "Just give me sufficient money // And please restore my health" from 'Lazarus' – "In fact, dear Lord, if you wouldn't mind" – in *From Now to Then*, p.22) will seem less unreasonable if one considers, for example, the effects of economic conditions after 1929 on the next two decades or so of history: "Would fascism have become very significant in world history but for the Great Slump? Probably not"

(Hobsbawm, *Age of Extremes*). During the worst period of the Slump in 1932–33, 44% of German workers were unemployed. After the Nazis came to power in 1933, they succeeded by a wide variety of means (one of the most important of which was rearmament) in becoming the only Western government to eliminate unemployment as a major problem. The relative importance attached to money and genocide in the '30s and '40s can perhaps be gauged from the fact that when details of the Final Solution began to reach the outside world during 1941–42, "throughout the process of discovery, the findings, when published, were seldom front-page news" (Hilberg). In other words, almost everyone "lacked the frame of mind and sense of urgency to address the Jewish fate…" – whereas "The Slump was front-page news" (*Stephanskirchen (1)*, p.55) as good as everywhere.

p.133 'The Happy Warrior': Wordsworth's remarkable poem, *Character of the Happy Warrior* (1807), presents the career of the "man in arms" not only as a vocation but, potentially, as one of the highest. Endowed with "an inward light / That makes the path before him always bright", exercising "a power / Which is our human nature's highest dower" – namely, to control, subdue and transmute pain, fear and bloodshed – Wordsworth's soldier

> Finds comfort in himself and in his cause;
> And, while the mortal mist is gathering, draws
> His breath in confidence of Heaven's applause…

One is reminded, it may be, of the third of Eliot's *Four Quartets*: "So Krishna, when he admonished Arjuna / On the field of battle." And yet, as with the *Bhagavad-Gita* – which can similarly be viewed, up to a point, as an expression of spiritual enlightenment but, in the context of the *Mahabarata*, serves the predominantly worldly purpose of overcoming the hero Arjuna's resistance to slaughtering his relatives in battle (*TLS*, Letters, 8 Sept. 2011) – Wordsworth's alarming misapplication of great ideas illustrates by default the importance of a compassionate *ethical* basis for even the most 'enlightened' states of mind or modes of action. In this respect, it seems that Joseph Brodsky's diagnosis of "unenlightened self-interest" may sometimes in fact apply to beliefs or behaviour which appear to be the very opposite (cp. note on p.55 **The Jews were *different*, etc.**, especially the last two paragraphs)… It was easier, perhaps, to deceive oneself then, in the English Lake District, than it ought to be in post-twentieth century Europe and America (where, however, variations on the early Christian idea of a 'just war' have been making a worrying re-appearance). Nevertheless, in less sheltered places than Grasmere, the early decades of the nineteenth century foreshadowed not only the disasters but some of the horrors of later history – as witnessed, for example, by Goya, who produced, between about 1810 and 1815 (i.e. only a few years after Wordsworth wrote his poem) his *Disastres de la Guerra* on the Spanish guerrilla war against the French. Whereas *Character of the Happy Warrior* simply fails to consider the morality or immorality – the justice or injustice – of either war in general or any war in particular, Goya constantly confronts the viewer with scenes which compel him to do just that – and to answer or admit that he *cannot* answer the same question, inscribed beneath one of the series' cruellest images, as Primo Levi asked the guard in Auschwitz: *Por qué* (Why?)... The belief that any war should only be fought in self-defence – and as a last resort, when all else has failed – is at least defensible, although "justified" or "justifiable" might be a less inflammatory and self-congratulatory epithet than just "just". It goes – or ought to go – without saying that the wholesale murder of civilians, or 'total war', is nothing but wholesale murder and, as such, indefensible.

p.133 **...gave rich and poor / The *Wirtschaftswunder*:** As Sebald and others have pointed out, forgetting (cp. **we *must* deceive ourselves, forget...**) was one of the prerequisites of the *Wirtschaftswunder*, as was the more or less deliberate cultivation of insensibility. In his quietly unnerving way, Sebald also lists: "the scrapping of outdated industrial complexes – an operation performed with brutal efficiency by the bomber squadrons – but also something less often acknowledged: the unquestioning work ethic learned in a totalitarian society, the logistical capacity for improvisation shown by a [war] economy under constant threat, experience in the use of 'foreign labour forces', and the lifting of the heavy burden of history that went up in flames between 1942 and 1945..." (*Air War and Literature*).

Much of the power of Sebald's writing derives from his unflinching ability to confront his readers with the sort of historical and psychological realities they might prefer to look away from even while looking, as he carefully puts it, at the same time as he calmly disarms most forms of objection with unanswerable arguments. As regards forgetting in general, though, Sebald himself seems sometimes to forget that the more or less consciously deceptive or self-deceptive variety is not the only one. Borges' little story, *Cain and Abel*, for example, in which the brothers cannot remember who killed whom, presents another argument which, if not unanswerable, is persuasive in its brevity: "Forgetting *is* forgiving." In day-to-day life, this may overlap with the implications of Yeats's vision in *The Second Coming* (cp. p.168): "The darkness drops again...". Or, as Emily Dickinson – a poet profoundly (self-)endowed with that "peculiar honesty, in a world too frightened to be honest" which

Eliot found in Blake – unforgettably wrote of remembering / forgetting:

> There is a pain – so utter –
> It swallows substance up –
> Then covers the Abyss with Trance –
> So Memory can step
> Around – across – upon it –
> As one within a Swoon –
> Goes safely – where an open eye –
> Would drop Him – Bone by Bone.

p.135   "It seems 131 towns and cities / Were bombed...":   From about 1940 onwards support for an all-out bombing campaign had been growing in the RAF and Churchill sent a much-quoted letter to Beaverbrook in the summer of that year hoping for "an absolutely devastating attack by very heavy bombers from this country on the Nazi homeland". In October the War Cabinet pronounced that "the civilian population around the target areas must be made to feel the weight of the war". This was already a weakening of the high principles with which the British had entered the war: shortly before the fighting began, Neville Chamberlain had instructed Bomber Command to restrict its activities to "legitimate military targets" which were to be "capable of identification". He told the House of Commons that the Air Ministry would "never resort to the deliberate attack on women and children, and other civilians, for the purpose of mere terrorism". However, by 1941 the Germans were at the height of their power and there was almost nothing the British *could* do apart from bomb. In February 1942, shortly before Arthur Harris became C-in-C of Bomber Command, so-called area bombing was approved by a Cabinet decision "to destroy the morale of the enemy civilian population and, in particular, of the industrial workers". The idea of area bombing – usually under cover of darkness – had developed because efforts at bombing specific targets were found to be suicidal by day, on account of highly effective German defences, and almost totally inaccurate by night. Voices were raised in protest on moral grounds at every stage, resulting in what has been called a "massive official war of lies": "In some ways area bombing was a three-year period of deceit practised on the British public and on world opinion" (Martin Middlebrook, *The Battle of Hamburg*, 1980). Churchill himself referred to the campaign as "moral bombing" – a formulation which continues to defy belief. But the nature of Harris's task seems to have been clear to him from the start and, after the tremendous success of 'Operation Gomorrah' or 'the Battle of Hamburg' (as Harris himself vaingloriously named it – together with the Battle of Berlin and the Battle of the Ruhr), he grew openly irritated with Churchill's unwillingness to endorse his tactics in public: "The aim of the Combined Bomber Offensive," he wrote, "should be unambiguously stated [to be] the destruction of German cities, the killing of German workers, and the destruction of civilized life throughout Germany." Or, more pugnaciously still, "the destruction of houses, public utilities, transport and lives, the creation of a refugee problem on an unprecedented scale, and the breakdown of morale both at home and at the battle fronts by fear of extended and intensified bombing, are accepted and intended aims of our bombing policy. They are not by-products of attempts to hit factories." The bombing of Hamburg in July 1943, resulting in the great *Feuersturm* (the word was coined to refer to it) of the night of the 27/28th – *die Katastrophe*, as the inhabitants of Hamburg still call it – was capable at the time of being defended, at least, as a strategic necessity. But 'Operation Thunderclap', or the utter destruction of fifteen square miles of the heavily populated historic centre of Dresden – one of the most beautiful cities in Europe – in February 1945 seems to have worried even Harris, who first of all opposed it as not worthwhile and later defended himself in *Bomber Offensive* by writing, "I know that the destruction of so large and splendid a city at this late stage of the war was considered unnecessary even by a good many people who admit that our earlier attacks were as fully justified as any other operation of war. Here I will only say that the attack on Dresden was at the time considered a military necessity by more important people than myself." Churchill attempted to disown Harris after the war, but earlier he had found himself caught in a trap of his own making: the government and the semi-controlled press had glorified 'Bomber' Harris and his aircrews, and it was impossible to get rid of him publicly even when he as good as refused to concentrate on industrial targets and kept 'browning' one city after another. Churchill had initiated the bombing of German civilians in order to destroy their morale and he knew, of course, from the beginning what was meant by this. The bother over Dresden seems to have worried him as well, however, and he sent a now notorious telegram (dated 28 March) to the British Chiefs of Staff and the Chief of the Air Staff: "It seems to me that the moment has come when the question of *bombing German cities simply for the sake of increasing the terror, though under other pretexts*, should be reviewed. Otherwise we shall come into control of an utterly ruined land… The Foreign Secretary has spoken to me on this subject and I feel the need for more precise concentration upon military objectives such as oil and communications behind the immediate battle-zone, rather than on *mere acts of terror and wanton destruction, however impressive*" (my italics). These "acts of terror" eventually resulted in the deaths of over 400,000 German civilians, if one finds that "impressive" – not to mention the sixty-out-of-a-hundred British airmen who were lost in the operations, leading Harris's own men to nickname him 'Butcher' or 'Butch' Harris.

p.136 My own 'synoptic, artificial view': So called by Sebald (*"einen synoptischen, künstlichen Blick"*, *Luftkrieg und Literatur*, p.33) because he attempts to go beyond the inevitably partial accounts of individual eyewitnesses to offer a more general view of the bombing of Hamburg, put together by himself. ***Out of* Niemandsland** is indebted again – as is Sebald – to Martin Middlebrook's pioneering work, *The Battle of Hamburg*, quoted above. As one would expect, many estimates and details vary or are disputed, but the first and worst firestorm of the war seems to have developed because of the unusually dry and warm weather, the accurate concentration of the bombing in one area, and the virtual impossibility of fighting the great number of fires which were started simultaneously by the lethal combination of high-explosive 'blockbusters' of up to 4,000 lb followed by incendiary bombs.

p.137 "I got no further": Or "That was a way of putting it", as Eliot put it in *East Coker* (1940) – a village in Somerset from which his seventeenth century ancestors had fled because of religious persecution to the New World, and in whose churchyard he saw "old stones that cannot be deciphered" marking graves which may have been those of even earlier, forgotten forebears… The Biblical quotation in ***Out of* Niemandsland** is from *Genesis XIX.24–28*. The problem of how to approach in writing such unimaginable events as the bombing of Hamburg is perhaps unresolvable, and "every attempt / … a different kind of failure". Nevertheless, in praising Hans Erich Nossack's description of the bombing in *Der Untergang* (The End), which was first published in 1948, Sebald says, "he was the only writer of the time to try recording what he actually saw as plainly as possible." *Der Untergang*, Sebald continues, is unique even in Nossack's own work. Moreover, "The ideal of truth inherent in its entirely unpretentious objectivity, at least over long passages, proves itself the only legitimate reason for continuing to produce literature in the face of total destruction. Conversely, the construction of aesthetic or pseudo-aesthetic effects from the ruins of an annihilated world is a process depriving literature of its right to exist."

p.140 As 'fire-gel' flared and clung – a form of napalm: Some survivors of the bombing have always claimed that phosphorus was used, particularly in the second phase of the attack, but this has been professionally disputed – for example, by the Dresden explosives expert, Thomas Langer, in Sebastian

Dehnhardt's documentary film, *Das Drama von Dresden* (ZDF, 2005). Langer uses the words *Brandgel* and *Feuergel* for the variety of incendiary which he believes was dropped (napalm itself had already been invented and named in the USA). Dehnhardt's documentary ends with a service of atonement in the Dresden *Frauenkirche*, which had at last been restored after its virtual destruction in the bombing. At about the same time, the British historian, Frederick Taylor, from whose book, *Dresden: Tuesday, February 13, 1945*, some of the quotations in these notes derive, said in an interview with *Der Spiegel*: "I personally find the attack on Dresden horrific. It was overdone, it was excessive and is to be regretted enormously." *Das Drama von Dresden* is not a great film. However, it includes some extraordinary testimony from survivors, and this section of the poem is indebted in particular to the memories and words of Gerda Birnbaum, Helmut Camphausen, Ursula Elsner, Werner Hanitzsch, Eleonora Kompisch, Leandro Marton-Karoly, Günther Reichel, Johannes Süß.

p.141 **His own self-portrait claimed:** Gray's *Elegy* is plainly enough – as the 'self-portrait as…' here claims – a self-portrait in a country churchyard:

> The curfew tolls the knell of parting day,
> The lowing herd winds slowly o'er the lea,
> The ploughman homeward plods his weary way,
> And leaves the world to darkness and to me.

On the other hand, Gray's identity within the poem is highly artificial and it is tempting, since the completed *Elegy* was not published until he was in his mid-thirties, to read it as a 'self-portrait as a young poet' in the country churchyard and then, towards its close, '…as a *dead* young poet' – a fascinating variation on the genre, rescued from proto-Romanticism not only by the degree of its artifice but by more than a suggestion of self-mockery:

> Here rests his head upon the lap of earth,
> A youth to fortune and to fame unknown…

Gray's poem is otherwise remarkable for its rejection of the belligerent assumptions which lay behind Dryden's two famous poems – on the death of Cromwell and *Annus Mirabilis* – in this verse-form, "which I have ever judg'd more noble, both for the sound and number, than any other Verse in use amongst us". If the lot of those buried in the country churchyard forbad greatness – "Some mute inglorious Milton here may rest, / Some

Cromwell guiltless of his country's blood" – it never tempted them either to make calculated use of terror, like Cromwell in Ireland:

> nor circumscribed alone
> Their growing virtues, but their crimes confined,
> Forbad to wade through slaughter to a throne,
> And shut the gates of mercy on mankind…

p.142 *'Wo wird einst des Wandermüden / Letzte Ruhestätte sein?'*: These are the lines from Heine's *Wo?* (Where?), inscribed on his gravestone in Montmartre, Paris, which are translated above, together with the end of his *Jetzt Wohin?*, in my note on p.28 **"As long as I've had my fun / I'll rest under any sod"**.

p.142 **"'How you take it'"**: A quotation from *The Tempest* used as the epigraph of the final section of 'The Dance of Death' in *Boccaccio in Florence and Other Poems* (p.27).

p.143 **As for what really happened**: Modern Biblical scholarship tends to the view that Jesus would have been unlikely to rebuke Martha for her hard work and hospitality and that the thirty or so years of oral tradition between his life and St Luke's account of it have somewhat upset the balance of what he meant… The Mary of the story has been identified in later Christian tradition with Mary Magdalen and she and Martha with the sisters of Lazarus, and though there is no evidence in support of these assumptions, the poem also makes them. At the end of ch.VII, Luke describes Mary Magdalen washing Jesus's feet with her tears and anointing them with oil. When Simon the Pharisee objects that she is a sinner, Jesus replies: "Her sins, which are many, are forgiven, for she loved much." To Mary herself he says, "Thy faith hath saved thee; go in peace" (vv. 47, 50). In other words, in Jesus's view, Mary was instantaneously saved *by herself*, albeit with his help, as Satan instantaneously fell: "I beheld Satan as lightning fall from heaven" (*Luke X.18*).

p.143 **Many, it's true, see work / As domination. Little Caesars**: Cp. the episode at the office of the *Irish Freeman* in *Ulysses* in which Professor MacHugh (a Dublin classicist) declares, "I speak the tongue of a race the acme of whose mentality is the maxim: time is money. Material domination. *Dominus!* Lord! Where is the spirituality? Lord Jesus! Lord Salisbury. A sofa in a westend club." In the discussion towards the end of *A Portrait of the Artist as a Young Man*, referred to above (in note on p.88 **"What is truth?"**), Cranly observes to Stephen Dedalus, " – It is a curious thing, do you know, … how your mind is supersaturated with the religion in which you say you disbelieve." And the same was true of Joyce. In *Ulysses*, MacHugh has already been rude about the Romans (who were, of course, the dominant power in Judaea at the time of Jesus):

> – What was their civilization? Vast, I allow: but vile. Cloacae: sewers. The Jews in the wilderness and on the mountaintop said: *It is meet to be here. Let us build an altar to Jehovah.* The Roman, like the Englishman who follows in his footsteps, brought to every new shore on which he set his foot (on our shore he never set it) only his cloacal obsession. He gazed about him in his toga and he said: *It is meet to be here. Let us construct a watercloset.*
> – They were nature's gentlemen, J.J. O'Molloy murmured. But we have also Roman law.
> – And Pontius Pilate was its prophet, professor MacHugh responded.

Roman civilization was the context in which Luke's version of Jesus's life was written as well as of the life itself. When, on the night of 18 July A.D.64, a fire broke out in Rome which burnt for a week and destroyed half the city, rumour blamed the Emperor Nero, who, "to divert suspicion from himself, looked for a scapegoat. His choice fell on the Christians, because, as Tacitus tells us…, they were already 'detested for their outrageous practices'" (G.B. Caird, *The Gospel of St Luke*). The Christians had been harried by the Jews, whom the Romans had so far treated with exceptional tolerance, and by their pagan neighbours, who saw their religion as "*antisocial* and *different*" (Caird, my italics) – not to say *unpatriotic*. As the grim persecution of the Christians which followed gradually abated, Luke addressed his gospel to a high-ranking Roman civil servant named Theophilus with the aim of showing not only that the representatives of Rome in Judaea had found Jesus innocent but that he had been "a figure of nobility, grace, and charm", whose teaching inspired the same qualities in those who followed him.

p.144 He asked which part of things, though treasured, corrupted / On earth: Cp. "Lay not up for yourselves treasures upon earth, where moth and rust doth corrupt,… But lay up for yourselves treasures in heaven… For where your treasure is there will your heart be also" (*Matthew VI. 19–21*).

p.144 both parts are good: At approximately one o'clock in the morning in Skin-the-Goat Fitzharris's cabman's shelter, Leopold Bloom discusses "the money question, which was at the back of everything, greed and jealousy, people never knowing when to stop", as opposed to Jewish practicality and the necessity of work – to which Stephen, still recovering from the excesses of Nighttown, manages to respond, "Count me out, ... meaning to work". Stephen and Bloom are, in this respect, a sort of modernist Mary and Martha. Stephen's words surprise Bloom, who takes it for granted that "All must work, have to, together. – I mean, of course, ... work in the widest possible sense. Also literary labour, not merely for the kudos of the thing." He sees this as a form of patriotism:

> You have every bit as much right to live by your pen in pursuit of your philosophy as the peasant has. What? You both belong to Ireland, the brain and the brawn. Each is equally important.
> – You suspect, Stephen retorted with a sort of a half-laugh, that I may be important because I belong to the *faubourg Saint Patrice* called Ireland for short.
> – I would go a step further, Mr Bloom insinuated.
> – But I suspect, Stephen interrupted, that Ireland must be important because it belongs to me.

In spite of Stephen's eloquence and Bloom's uncomprehending clichés, one can fairly easily imagine the latter, in later years, remarking to the former, as Johannes Fest remarked to his son Joachim (see p.168), "You weren't wrong, but I was the one who was right." And if this inverts the referents, so be it. Another version of the same relationship was proposed by Jesus himself in answer to the question, "Is it lawful for us to give tribute to Caesar, or no?", namely: "Show me a penny. Whose image and superscription hath it? They answered and said, Caesar's. And he said unto them, Render therefore unto Caesar the things which be Caesar's, and unto God the things which be God's" (*Luke XX. 22, 24–25*).

p.144 **right work**: 'Right Means of Livelihood' is the fifth branch of the Buddha's Noble Eightfold Path Leading to the Cessation of Suffering. In the Buddha's teaching the *karma* of the moral life ("It is choice or intention that I call *karma* – mental work –, for having chosen a man acts by body, speech and mind") leads to or enables – is indeed inseparable from – the spiritual life. The third branch of the Eightfold Path is 'Right Speech' and the fourth is 'Right Action': cp. **we need to believe / In what we do**, etc.

p.144 **We need to absolve / Ourselves from our 'devices'**: Cp. note on p.51 **The German landscape Primo Levi / Found "rich and civilized"**, which refers to the General Confession in *The Book of Common Prayer* ('Morning Prayer' and 'Evening Prayer'): "Almighty and most merciful Father; We have erred, and strayed from thy ways like lost sheep. We have followed too much the devices and desires of our own hearts…"

p.145 **As the Son / Of Man, he neither lost nor won**: Jesus himself seems to have been fond of such conundrums, which bear a relationship to the *mantras* and *koans* of other religions. Memorable examples recorded by Luke are:

> Woe unto you when all men shall speak well of you (*VI.26*).

> Give to every man that asketh of thee; and of him that taketh away thy goods ask them not again (*VI.30*).

> For whosoever will save his life shall lose it; but whosoever will lose his life for my sake the same shall save it (*IX.24*).

> And behold there are last which shall be first and there are first which shall be last (*XIII.30*).

Of course, he could also speak with admirable directness:

> Take heed, and beware of covetousness; for a man's life consisteth not in the abundance of the things which he possesseth (*XII.15*).

p.147 *Epilogue: Rilke – In the Same River Twice*: "The doctrine that everything is in a state of flux is the most famous of the opinions of Heraclitus… 'You cannot step into the same river twice; for fresh waters are always flowing in upon you'" (Bertrand Russell, *History of Western Philosophy*). Of course, 'you' are never the same either, and Heraclitus also said: "We step and do not step into the same rivers: we are, and are not." As Russell notes, "there would be no unity if there were not opposites to combine". Thus Heraclitus "contains the germ" of Hegel's dialectic, "which proceeds by a synthesis of opposites"… Context, at any rate, affects the meaning of poetry as much as that of any other utterance, and the *Epilogue* reproduces with alternative readings two poems translated in *Boccaccio in Florence*. Rudolf **Kassner** was an eclectic essayist of whom Rilke thought highly enough to make him the dedicatee of his Eighth *Duino Elegy* – on the nature of human consciousness. *Wendung* (here translated as 'Turn') was written on 20 June 1914. In late 1905 Rilke had spent a day at Chartres together with Rodin. On the south side of the cathedral there is a sculpture of an angel holding a sun-dial, on which Rilke fixed his gaze as a thunderstorm approached and then broke… The summer of 1914 – as Rilke could not have known when he wrote his poems – took, of course, another sort of turn and was the start of an infinitely more terrible because more human storm. Over the thirty-one years of world conflict which followed there were moments, as Eric Hobsbawm wrote at the beginning of the first chapter of *Age of Extremes*, "when the end of a considerable proportion of the human race did not look far off. There were surely times when the god or gods, whom pious humans believed to have created the world and all in it, might have been expected to regret having done so."

p.147 ***Long had he triumphed by looking***: As a number of the poems by Rilke translated in *Boccaccio in Florence* go to show, Rilke was in some respects a literary precursor of the 'existentialist' philosophers, Heidegger and Sartre, and the former refers to him in his writings (George Steiner, *Heidegger*, 1992). In Pt III of *Being and Nothingness* (1943) Sartre devotes an entire chapter (*The Look*) to the power of people's looks over one another – and goes on to consider the limits of that power, since one cannot "capture a 'consciousness'" or "possess a freedom". Sartre's view (expounded in Pt III.3.I of his book) that "Conflict is the original meaning of Being-for-others" is well known. *In the Same River Twice* and other sections of *Afterwords* suggest, however, more than one way out of the hell of his *In Camera*, brilliant though it is. Of which more in *Opus 3*.